Analysing Financial Statements for Non-Specialists

All business organizations produce financial statements and the information communicated (or hidden) on these has never been more important to understand following the global financial crisis.

Analysing Financial Statements for Non-Specialists introduces this topic without assuming prior training and study in accounting – as such, it is perfect for students and managers who need to build their understanding of financial statements without taking an entire degree in accounting.

With features such as end-of-chapter questions, topics for further discussion and brimming with real-world examples, this concise new textbook provides a comprehensive resource that will be welcomed by lecturers and instructors charged with delivering classes on financial statements.

Jim O'Hare is Principal Teaching Fellow at the University of Leicester, UK. His research interests are on the usefulness of company financial statements and their use in making economic decisions.

Analysing Financial Statements for Non-Specialists

Jim O'Hare

Routledge
Taylor & Francis Group

LONDON AND NEW YORK

First published 2013
by Routledge
2 Park Square, Milton Park, Abingdon, Oxon OX14 4RN

Simultaneously published in the USA and Canada
by Routledge
711 Third Avenue, New York, NY 10017

Routledge is an imprint of the Taylor & Francis Group, an informa business

British Library Cataloguing in Publication Data
A catalogue record for this book is available from the British Library

Library of Congress Cataloging in Publication Data
O'Hare, Jim.
  Analysing financial statements for non-specialists/Jim O'Hare.
  p. cm.
  Includes bibliographical references and index.
  1. Financial statements. I. Title.
  HF5681.B2O33 2012
  332.63'2042–dc23
  2012024558

ISBN: 978-0-415-62472-5 (hbk)
ISBN: 978-0-415-62473-2 (pbk)
ISBN: 978-0-203-10430-9 (ebk)

Typeset in Times New Roman and Gill Sans
by Florence Production, Stoodleigh, Devon

MIX
Paper from
responsible sources
FSC
www.fsc.org   FSC® C004839

Printed and bound in Great Britain by
TJ International Ltd, Padstow, Cornwall

Contents

Chapter 1

Why is analysing financial statements necessary?

1.1 Why do companies have to prepare and publish their accounts?

For many years, limited liability companies have been owned and managed by two different groups of people. The owners are the shareholders and the managers are the directors. Because of this separation it became necessary for information to be produced by the management as a report to the owners. This report is needed to demonstrate how well the management have looked after the investment of the owners; this is usually referred to as their 'stewardship' role. The report produced is what we now refer to as the 'annual report and accounts' or 'financial statements'. This has now been the case for hundreds of years, and the need for accurate and honest reporting was highlighted as early as the eighteenth century by the first great financial scandal – 'The South Sea Bubble'.

The South Sea Company was formed in 1711 to trade, mostly in slaves, with Spanish America. Following what turned out to be over-optimistic forecasts of growth, in 1720, the stock in the company boomed and the company grew to the extent that it actually took over the national debt. The market then collapsed (stock prices fell from over £1,000 to less than £100), leading to a House of Commons inquiry that showed that three ministers had accepted bribes, and the company directors were disgraced.

The scandal brought Robert Walpole to power as prime minister and led to increased regulation of companies. The South Sea Company actually survived this crisis and continued to trade until 1853.

From that time until very recently, the financial statements produced by the management of a company were seen as only being relevant to that company's shareholders. It is only in very recent times that it has been accepted that groups and individuals other than the owners do use the information in those financial statements. This acceptance has led the International Accounting Standards Board (IASB) to recognize a change in the way they define the objective of financial statements.

Previous attempts by various bodies to define the purpose and objective of company financial statements always referred to the need to give information to shareholders, and only shareholders. It was not until late in the twentieth century that it was formally recognized that there were many other users of the financial statements.

In recent years, a lot of time and effort has been put into developing a 'framework of principles' to guide the development of preparing company financial statements. This framework aims to answer these questions:

* What is the objective of financial statements?
* Who are the users of financial statements?
* What are the important qualitative characteristics of financial statements?
* What should financial statements contain and how should the contents be defined and measured?

The first 'framework' was probably the one developed by the Financial Accounting Standards Board (FASB) in the United States of America in 1973. In 1975 in the UK, the Institute of Chartered Accountants in England and Wales (ICAEW) produced 'The Corporate Report', which 'aimed to be the starting point for a major review of the users, purposes and methods of modern financial reporting'.

The more recently formed IASB drew on the work previously done in both the UK and the USA when it produced the 'Framework for the Preparation and Presentation of Financial Statements', which defined the objective of financial statements as:

> to provide information about the financial position, performance and changes in financial position of an enterprise that is useful to a wide range of users in making economic decisions.

The framework was first published in 1989 but not adopted by the IASB until 2001.

It is very important that anyone who prepares financial statements should now recognize the range of potential users who may use them to make economic decisions. If the information in the financial statements turned out to be incorrect, then it is now thought possible that any of the users could make a claim for damages if they had suffered a loss as a result of such inaccuracies. Previously it was considered that only shareholders could take such an action.

1.2 Who are the users of financial statements and what economic decisions do they need to make?

Some of the user groups are:

1   Shareholders – both existing and potential shareholders need information to enable them to make decisions relating to buying or selling shares in a company. The financial statements of a company will contain information that will help with this decision. For example, it will give information about the amount of dividend paid to shareholders; if the dividend is high, this will suit shareholders who need income, but may not suit those who want growth in their investment.

2 Lenders such as banks need to be able to assess whether any loans that they have made or are about to make are safe. The financial statements can be used to see if the company is generating sufficient profits to meet the repayments on a loan or if they have sufficient assets that the lender could hold as security for the loan.

3 Suppliers to a company will usually supply goods and services on credit. They may deliver their goods or provide a service several weeks before they get paid. The financial statements will enable these suppliers to assess whether the company that they are about to supply is likely to have the funds available to pay for the goods and services when that payment falls due.

4 Customers need to know if they are being overcharged for what they are buying and whether they can rely on receiving goods or services into the future. The financial statements may show if the company they are buying from is making excessive profits and whether they might fail in the future.

5 Employees and trade union groups will also use financial statements. Existing employees need information to be able to make realistic claims for a pay rise and potential employees will be concerned about the potential failure of the company.

6 The government will use data in company financial statements for many purposes, not least the need for the tax authorities to assess the amount of tax payable on profits made.

The above list does not cover all of the potential users, nor does it refer to all of the potential economic decisions that may be made by those users. We can only conclude that there is a very wide range of users who make different types of economic decision. The following chapters will address the ways in which the users can analyse the financial statements in order to make their decisions.

1.3 What are the required characteristics of useful financial information?

All of the user groups will need to be able to understand the content of the financial statements, to compare different entities and to rely on the data in those statements. The IASB framework describes the following 'qualitative characteristics of useful financial information'.

1 Relevance – the information given in the financial statements should be capable of affecting the decisions made by the users. For this to be possible, the information should be useful in making predictions or confirming values or both.

2 Faithful representation – the information reported in the financial statements should be complete, unbiased and free from error.

3 Comparability – the information will be of more use if it can be compared to similar information about other entities and from other time periods. This should allow the user to identify and understand differences, and similarities, between entities and over time.

4 Verifiability – the information should faithfully represent the financial performance and position of the entity. Verifiability means that if a number of qualified and independent users reviewed the information they could reach a consensus that the information gives a faithful representation.

5   Timeliness – it is important that users receive the information in time for it to have an impact on any decisions to be made.

6   Understandability – presenting the information in a clear and concise way will help to make it more understandable. Some of the information disclosed in financial statements will be complex. It would be misleading if this complex information was left out; therefore, it must be assumed that users of financial statements will have a reasonable knowledge of business and will take care when analysing the information.

1.4 The content of financial statements

The financial statements produced by an entity are a representation of all of the financial transactions that have occurred in a period – usually a year. The effects of these transactions can be grouped together and these 'groups' are called 'elements of financial statements'. There are five elements in financial statements. Three of these elements – assets, liabilities and equity – help to describe the financial position of a company and are represented in a 'balance sheet' or 'statement of financial position' (two different names for the same thing, which happens a lot in accountancy). The other two elements, income and expenses, are related to financial performance and are represented in an 'income statement' or 'profit and loss account'.

The framework defines the elements as follows:

- **Asset** – An asset is a resource controlled by the entity as a result of past events and from which future economic benefits are expected to flow to the entity.

> An example of an asset would be a machine that a company has bought. As the owner (the past event would be the purchase of the machine), the company would control its use and the machine may be used to produce goods that could be sold to create an economic benefit (or profit).
>
> As the definition uses the word 'controlled' and not 'owned', we would also include as assets resources that are not legally owned. For example, a machine that is on a long lease and will spend most of its useful life with the entity but is legally owned by the lessor is treated as an asset of the lessee. This is an example of accounting for the 'substance' of a transaction over its legal form, an important concept in accountancy.

- **Liability** – A liability is a present obligation of the entity arising from past events, the settlement of which is expected to result in an outflow from the entity of resources embodying economic benefits.

> An example of a liability would be a bank loan. As the entity had been given funds by a bank in the past it now has an obligation to repay it. The outflow would be the cash used to repay it.

> The outflow to settle a liability will not always be cash. If a customer has paid in advance for some service from an entity that has not yet been provided, then the entity will have an 'obligation' to provide that service in the future and that would be classified as a liability.

- **Equity** – Equity is the residual interest in the assets of the entity after deducting all its liabilities.

> Equity can also be referred to as the 'ownership interest' in an entity. It links to the assets and liabilities in the 'accounting equation':
>
> Assets – Liabilities = Equity
>
> The accounting equation is represented by a balance sheet. On one side we have assets minus liabilities, which 'balances' with the other side, equity.

- **Income** – Income is increases in economic benefits during the accounting period in the form of inflows or enhancements of assets, or decreases in liabilities, that result in increases in equity, other than those relating to contributions from equity participants.

> The sales a company makes are its main source of 'income'. They result, usually, in an inflow of cash to the entity.
>
> A discount received by a supplier will also be 'income' as it will result in a reduction of the amount owed to that supplier (decrease in a liability).
>
> If a company issues some shares to generate cash, then that cash is not classified as 'income' as the shareholder is an 'equity participant'.

- **Expense** – Expenses are decreases in economic benefits during an accounting period in the form of outflows or depletions of assets or incurrences of liabilities that result in decreases in equity, other than those relating to distributions to equity participants.

> If a company pays an electricity bill, this results in an 'expense' as a result of the reduction of the asset of cash. An expense will also reduce profits and this in turn will reduce equity. Depreciation of assets (see Chapter 2) also results in an 'expense'. However, when a company pays a dividend to its shareholders, that outflow is not classified as an 'expense' as it is a distribution to equity participants.

Assets, liabilities, income and expenses are included in the financial statements when it is 'probable' that economic benefits will flow and they can be measured reliably. Accountants take a rather prudent view when assessing probability in that they are more likely to include liabilities and expenses when there is a doubt about the outflow of economic benefit than they would be to include assets and income.

Most transactions are recorded at their 'historic cost', meaning that we record them at their value at the time of the transaction and not their value at the balance sheet date.

- An entity that holds some inventory that was bought several months ago may have made a holding gain. The replacement value of the goods may have risen since the time of purchase but the company will not recognize that gain in its financial statements.

Problems

1   Do the following meet the IASB definition of an asset?
    (a) A customer who owes a company money.
    (b) A company car used by a director.
    (c) A computer used for administration purposes.
2   Which elements are affected when a football club buys a player for £30m? Is the footballer an asset?
3   Tick the appropriate boxes to show which elements would change as a result of the transactions in the left-hand column – more than one is usually affected and in some cases it will be 'either/or'.

	Asset	Liability	Equity	Income	Expense
Buy a new machine					
Buy goods on credit					
Issue new shares					
Sell goods for more than they cost for cash					
Purchase some stationery					
Purchase some goods for resale					
Receive a bill for tax					
Take out a bank loan					
Pay bank interest					
Pay cheque into bank					
Make a lease payment					
Pay some dividends					

Activity

1   Make a list of the range of possible economic decisions that each of the six user groups mentioned in this chapter might make.

Discussion topics

1   Is it right that accountants include assets in the balance sheet of a company that they do not legally own?

2   Should the elements shown in the financial statements reflect their current value rather than their original cost?

Chapter 2

What information is provided in company financial statements?

In Chapter 1 we established that accounting transactions lead to groups of elements that are called assets, liabilities, equity, income and expenses. In this chapter we will look in more detail at exactly what we are likely to find in a set of financial statements within each of those elements.

2.1 Assets

Assets are divided into two categories in a set of financial statements. We have non-current (or 'fixed') assets and current assets. Accountancy can be confusing because the same word can sometimes be used to mean different things, and there can be different words or phrases that mean the same thing. Here the term 'non-current assets' is the same as 'fixed assets'. In the UK, the term 'fixed assets' is still used by unquoted companies preparing their financial statements under 'UK GAAP' (generally accepted accounting practice), but the introduction of International Accounting Standards has led to the change to 'non-current' – probably because it translates more precisely into other languages. This book is based on the international terminology but will give the UK GAAP equivalents where appropriate.

2.1.1 Non-current assets

An asset is 'non-current' if it is of a material value and will generate economic benefits in more than one accounting period – meaning that they cost a lot of money and last a long time!

How much is 'material'? That will depend on the size of the company – in a small company £1,000 may be a significant sum, whereas many large companies prepare their financial statements to the nearest million, so the 'materiality' level would be set a lot higher for those companies.

Money spent acquiring non-current assets is referred to as 'capital expenditure' and all other purchases will be referred to as 'revenue expenditure'. The distinction is not always clear. Some expenditure will clearly always be capital – for example, when a company buys a new building for £2m and some will always be revenue, as when a company buys some materials to be used in production of goods for resale. Some expenditure can be either – for example, a new computer may be regarded as of material value and having a long life by one company, therefore classed as capital expenditure, but not by another, who classes it as revenue expenditure.

The distinction between capital and revenue expenditure is important because of the accounting treatment of each. Capital expenditure is spread out over the useful life of the asset; this is what accountants refer to as 'depreciation', whereas revenue expenditure is accounted for in the period in which it is incurred.

Example 2.1

A company spends £100,000:

- If treated as capital expenditure with a useful life of five years, there could be an expense (depreciation) of £20,000 a year for each of those five years – profit will be reduced by that amount each year.
- If treated as revenue expenditure, there will be an expense of £100,000 in that first year and nothing for the next four years. There will be a large impact on profit in one year and none in the future.
- Two different companies could treat the same expenditure in different ways.

2.1.2 Depreciation

Depreciation is the spreading of the cost of a non-current asset over its useful life. It is not used to reflect the value of the asset. All non-current assets with a useful life (only freehold land is, usually, considered to go on forever) have to be depreciated even if their current value is increasing. Buildings should be depreciated.

Accounting standards only refer to the cost being spread 'as fairly as possible' and this can, again, lead to different companies treating the same expenditure in different ways.

Example 2.2

- A non-current asset is purchased for £60,000 and has a life of three years, at which time it is expected to have a 'residual' value of £20,580. That means that the net cost of £39,000 (64,000 – 25,000) has to be spread out over the three-year life of the asset.
- Spreading the cost evenly over the useful life is known as the 'straight line method' and that would give depreciation of £13,140 each year.
- Depreciation could also be calculated by taking the same proportion of the remaining value each year – say, 30 per cent, so in the first year we have depreciation of £18,000 (30 per cent of 60,000) and then the next year we have depreciation of £12,600 (30 per cent of 60,000 – 18,000). This is known as the 'reducing balance method'.

Table 2.1 shows that we get a different depreciation expense each year, but over the useful life of the asset the impact is the same. These are only two of many different methods of accounting for depreciation but are the two most commonly used in practice.

In their financial statements companies do not tell the user what method of depreciation they have applied but will state what they regard to be the useful lives of each category of non-current assets.

Table 2.1

	Straight line method £	Reducing balance method £
Initial cost	60,000	60,000
Depreciation in 1st year	13,140	18,000
Net book value (NBV) after 1 year	47,860	42,000
Depreciation in 2nd year	13,140	12,600
NBV after 2 years	34,720	29,400
Depreciation in 3rd year	13,140	8,820
NBV after 3 years	20,580	20,580

2.1.3 Tangible, intangible and investments

Non-current assets are divided into subcategories: 'tangible', 'intangible' and 'investments'. Tangible non-current assets are usually referred to as 'property, plant and equipment' – they can be seen and touched, they are tangible in nature. Intangible non-current assets meet the definition of an asset (see Chapter 1) and the definition of capital expenditure (see above) but cannot be seen or touched. The term 'amortization' is used for intangible non-current assets, rather than depreciation, to reflect the spreading of their cost over their useful lives.

* A company spends £2m on the development of a new product that will be sold over the next five years. The expenditure is material and will lead to economic benefits in more than one accounting period, but all that the company have, physically, are some pieces of paper showing the development plans. The £2m will be amortized over the five-year period when the product is sold.

Non-current asset investments are investments in other companies that are significant in value and are not held with the intention of resale in the short term.

Non-current assets are normally shown in the financial statements at a value of their cost less any accumulated depreciation to date – their 'net book value'. They can be revalued, however, to show increases in value to reflect permanent gains. This is commonly done for land and buildings but rarely done for other non-current assets. The revaluation will be reflected in a 'revaluation reserve' being created; this is shown as part of the equity of a company in its financial statements.

Non-current assets include:

* tangible: land and buildings, machinery, plant, vehicles, equipment, furniture, fixtures and fittings;
* intangible: goodwill, development expenditure, patents and royalties.

Goodwill is a measure of the value of the reputation of an entity. A company with a good reputation has an asset that will generate future economic benefits. Although known to exist, the goodwill that a company builds itself ('inherent' goodwill) is never included in its financial statements. Goodwill can only be included if it has been 'purchased'.

- Company A pays £30m for all of the shares in Company B, whose net assets have a fair value of £20m. The assets would transfer to Company A at their fair value and the other £10m is shown as goodwill.

A company can treat development costs as capital expenditure, but research costs are always treated as expenses in the year they arise. We capitalize development expenditure if there is a clearly defined project that is expected to result in future gains:

- A car manufacturer spends £10m developing a new model that will be sold over the next five years. The cost will be treated as an intangible non-current asset and will be spread (amortized) over the five-year period.

The data in Table 2.2 have been extracted from the 2012 annual report of Next plc. The table shows the net book values at the balance sheet date (in this case, 28 January 2012) for each category. The tangible assets are shown as 'property, plant and equipment'. The investments are the 'interests in associates' (an associate company is one in which the reporting company has a significant influence but not overall control) and 'other investments'. The 'defined benefit pension surplus' is the amount that the current value of the company pension fund exceeds the estimated future liability (in 2010 it was a deficit shown under non-current liabilities).

Much more detail is given in the notes to the accounts. In Table 2.3, the note for property, plant and equipment shows exactly what movements there have been over the last year.

Further information is disclosed in the 'accounting policies', which form part of the financial statements. This disclosure relates to the useful lives of each category of non-current assets and for Next plc it is shown in Table 2.4.

We can conclude from the data in Table 2.3 and the other notes to the financial statements that:

- There have been no acquisitions of property.
- No assets have been revalued in the last financial year.
- The property has not been depreciated.
- On average, 61 per cent (901.9/1483.8) of the useful life of the non-current assets has been 'used', which may suggest that some of the assets are getting near to the end of their useful lives. However, there is a further note that tells us that the company had entered into contracts to spend a further £9.5m on property, plant and equipment at the balance sheet date.
- There has been a lot of investment in plant and fittings.

We do not know:

- The method of depreciation.
- Why there is no depreciation of property.

Table 2.2

Non-current assets	2012 £m	2011 £m
Property, plant and equipment	581.9	592.4
Intangible assets	45.6	46.5
Interests in associates	6.1	5.1
Other investments	1.0	1.0
Defined benefit pension surplus	35.1	55.7
Other financial assets	44.6	24.3
	714.3	725.0

Table 2.3

	Freehold property £m	Leasehold property £m	Plant and fittings £m	Total £m
Cost				
At January 2011	74.3	8.3	1,352.6	1,435.2
Exchange movement			(0.2)	(0.2)
Additions			126.1	126.1
Disposals	(0.8)		(28.9)	(29.7)
Disposal of subsidiaries			(47.6)	(47.6)
At January 2012	73.5	8.3	1,402.0	1,483.8
Depreciation				
At January 2011	8.3	1.4	833.1	842.8
Exchange movement			(0.1)	(0.1)
Provided during the year			118.8	118.8
Impairment charge			1.4	1.4
Disposals	(0.1)		(23.2)	(23.3)
Disposal of subsidiaries			(37.7)	(37.7)
At January 2012	8.2	1.4	892.3	901.9
Carrying amount at January 2012	65.3	6.9	509.7	581.9

Table 2.4

Freehold and long leasehold property	50 years
Plant, machinery and building works	10–25 years
Fixtures and fittings	6–15 years
Vehicles, IT and other assets	2–6 years
Leasehold improvements	The period of the lease or useful life if shorter

2.1.4 Current assets

Current assets are short-term assets and include:

- inventory (or stock);
- receivables (or debtors);
- investments;
- cash and cash equivalents.

Inventory represents raw materials awaiting use in manufacture or service, work in progress (items in the manufacturing process but not completed yet) and finished goods awaiting sale. We value these items at the lower of what they cost and their 'net realizable value'.

- Cost is taken as the cost of bringing the goods to their present location and condition. For manufacturing companies, the cost of finished goods will include the cost of materials, labour and an apportionment of relevant overheads.
- Net realizable value of an item is its selling price less any costs that will be directly incurred in selling it (packaging, delivery costs, commission, etc.).

This method of valuation is another example of the prudent way in which financial statements are prepared. No profit is taken for the sale of an item until it is actually sold – profits cannot be anticipated but losses can. For example, if we buy an item for £10 and plan to sell it for £15, we cannot account for the profit (£5) until it is sold, but if we believe that it can only be sold for £6, then we account for the loss (£4) immediately.

Receivables are usually separated into 'trade receivables' and 'other receivables'. Trade receivables are monies owed to an entity by its customers for goods sold to them on credit terms. Any amounts not thought to be collectable will not be included so that the figure shown in the financial statements is the minimum amount collectable.

Other receivables include other amounts owed to an entity – for example, some companies make short-term loans to employees or sub-let part of their premises. Prepayments are also included here; these relate to payments for expense items that have been made in advance.

Example 2.3

- A company with a financial year end of 31 March pays an insurance premium of £1.2m in January that covers the year to the 31 December.
- At the date of the balance sheet the company has only used three months (£0.3m) of the insurance and so only that part is included as an expense in the income statement.
- The other nine months (£0.9m) is 'prepaid'.
- Just as materials that have been bought but not yet used are classed as an asset (inventory), so are expenses that have been paid for but not used (prepayments).

Current asset investments are investments that are being held for the short term, probably to gain some return on a cash surplus while a longer-term use is sought for the funds invested.

Cash and cash equivalents will include bank balances and any cash held by an entity (till floats etc.) as well as deposits that can be turned into cash without notice.

The data in Table 2.5 have been extracted from the 2012 annual report of Next plc.

Table 2.5

Current assets	2012 £m	2011 £m
Inventories	371.9	368.3
Trade and other receivables	699.1	645.6
Other financial assets	12.5	4.1
Cash and short-term deposits	56.4	49.3
	1,139.9	1,067.3

The notes to the financial statements tell us that:

- 97 per cent of the inventories are finished goods – there is a small amount of raw materials, work in progress and property development stocks.
- During the year the cost of inventories was reduced by £79.4m to restate those goods at their net realizable value.
- Trade receivables thought to be uncollectable amounted to £29.9m, but this was partly offset by a recovery of £3.3m of those written off in previous years.
- Trade receivables after deducting irrecoverable debts were £701.7m, but his figure was reduced by a £113.7m allowance for those debts considered to be 'doubtful' (over 16 per cent). £56.4m of receivables were over 120 days past being due, but this was an improvement from £61.2m the previous year.
- Most 'other receivables' were prepayments of £90.5m.
- Other financial assets were derivatives used to hedge against exchange and interest rate risks. A derivative is a security, the value of which depends on (is derived from) another asset.

Example 2.4

- A company is owed $2m by a customer that is due to be received in three months.
- If the current exchange rate is $1.5 to £1, the company will expect the amount due to realize £1.333m (2/1.5).
- If the exchange rate rises to $1.75 to £1 in three months, the amount due will only be £1.111m: an exchange loss of over £200k.
- To protect itself, the company could buy an asset that moves in line with the exchange rate, a 'financial future'. If the exchange rate rises, the value of this asset rises and the gain will offset the exchange loss.
- If the exchange rate falls, this gives rise to a financial liability, but the liability would be offset by an exchange gain.

2.2 Liabilities

Liabilities are divided (like assets) into non-current (sometimes described as 'long term') and current. Within each there are three types: liabilities, provisions and contingencies.

- With a liability we know exactly how much will be paid (or the value of economic benefit to be transferred) and when it needs to be paid by. So if a company buys goods on credit and agrees to pay in thirty days, or if money is borrowed from a bank and it is agreed to repay it over a ten-year period, then we have a liability.
- We call it a provision when there is a liability but the amount and/or the timing is uncertain. If a company rents some property, the terms of the lease agreed usually require that when the lease is over the property will be in the same condition that it was when the lease was taken out – therefore, they know that at some point in the future they will have a liability to carry out this work, but will not know exactly how much it will cost.
- A contingent liability is one that only arises depending on some future event. If a company is being sued by an unhappy customer for damages, the company only has a liability if they lose the case. Contingent liabilities are only included in the balance sheet if they are likely to result in a payment, although if unlikely, there is still a reference to them in the notes to the financial statements.

There is a much clearer distinction between non-current and current liabilities than with non-current and current assets. Non-current liabilities are those that are due for payment more than one year after the date of the balance sheet, and current liabilities are those that are due within that year.

- A ten-year bank loan will be a non-current liability, but if a part of the loan is due to be repaid within the next year, that part is classified as current.
- In the UK, tax on company profits is due nine months and one day after he date of the balance sheet, so will be a current liability. However, the accounting rules for calculating profit are not the same as the tax rules, and this sometimes leads to tax payments being made long after the accounting profit is recorded – this delayed tax payment is referred to as 'deferred tax'.

Liabilities include:

- borrowings;
- trade payables (or creditors) – these mainly consist of amounts due to those who have supplied goods and services on credit terms;
- other payables – includes 'accruals', which are expenses that have been incurred but have not yet been paid; most utility bills to companies are paid in arrears;
- tax and deferred tax;
- bank overdrafts – which should always be current as they are usually repayable on demand;
- provisions;
- contingent liabilities.

The data in Tables 2.6 and 2.7 have been extracted from the 2012 annual report of Next plc.

Table 2.6

Non-current liabilities	2012 £m	2011 £m
Corporate bonds	652.1	471.2
Provisions	12.0	13.3
Deferred tax liabilities	15.4	23.4
Other financial liabilities	4.4	2.6
Other liabilities	205.2	216.5
	889.1	727.0

Table 2.7

Current liabilities	2012 £m	2011 £m
Bank loans and overdrafts	7.6	125.2
Trade and other payables	545.0	544.6
Other financial liabilities	87.0	54.7
Current tax liabilities	102.8	108.4
	742.4	832.9

The notes to the financial statements give us further information on these balances:

- The corporate bonds are repayable 2013 (£89.9m), 2016 (£218.8m) and 2021 (£343.4m).
- Other non-current liabilities relate mainly to lease incentives received that will be credited to income after more than one year.
- Provisions relate to future exit costs of leases.
- Trade and other payables include 'trade payables' of £193.1m, 'other tax and social security' of £61.6m and 'other creditors and accruals' (not specified what they are, but a note tells us that they are not interest bearing) of £275.1m.

2.3 Equity

Equity represents the ownership interest in a company. It can be made up of the following:

- Share capital – this is the par value of the shares issued by the company to date. Next plc had over 168 million shares of 10p each in issue in January 2012. This value does not reflect the market value of the shares.

- Share premium account – this represents the amount above the par value that was paid by the shareholder when the shares were issued. If Next plc issued a share for £2, then 10p would be added to share capital and £1.90 added to the share premium account.
- Retained earnings – represents the accumulation of profits (or losses) that have been reinvested in the company rather than being returned to the shareholders as dividends.
- Revaluation reserves – the amount added to non-current assets to reflect their current value.
- Other reserves – companies can have a variety of different reserves.

The data in Table 2.8 have been extracted from the 2012 annual report of Next plc.

Table 2.8

Equity	2012	2011
	£m	£m
Share capital	16.9	18.1
Share premium account	0.8	0.8
Capital redemption reserve	13.0	11.8
ESOT reserve	(141.1)	(138.6)
Fair value reserve	11.5	(3.2)
Foreign currency translation reserve	2.0	4.6
Other reserves	(1,443.8)	(1,443.8)
Retained earnings	1,763.4	1,782.6
Non-controlling interest	–	0.1
	222.7	232.4

The notes to the financial statements also tell us that:

- The company is authorized to issue up to 400.5 million shares.
- That nearly 20 million shares, with a par value of 5p, were purchased from shareholders during the year and then cancelled.
- The negative, other reserves, comprise a reserve created on the reduction of share capital.
- ESOT is the Next 'Employee Share Ownership Trust', which provides for the issue of shares to group employees.

Movements in the equity from one year to another are seen as important to the users of financial statements. This has led to the introduction of an additional table called a 'Statement of Changes in Equity' (SOCIE). This statement shows all the movements in each of the headings under equity.

The SOCIE for a company may look like the (made up) example in Table 2.9.

Table 2.9

	Share capital £m	Share premium £m	Revaluation reserve £m	Retained earnings £m	Total equity £m
At December 2011	100	400	200	300	1,000
Profit for the year				250	250
Shares issued	10	50			60
Revaluation of non-current assets			50		50
Equity dividends paid				(100)	(100)
At December 2012	110	450	250	450	1,260

2.4 The balance sheet

The balance sheet, or 'statement of financial position', of a company is a representation of the accounting equation:

Assets – Liabilities = Equity

It represents a 'snapshot' of the assets and liabilities of the company at a particular point in time. A moment later the balances may have changed. The date for the financial statements is chosen by the company. If companies have different accounting year-end dates, this can lead to problems in comparing them, especially where trade is subject to seasonal variations. For example, a toy retailing company may show a larger-than-average inventory if the balance sheet date is in November, but it is likely to show a much lower inventory figure if the balance sheet date is in February.

A pro forma balance sheet based on International Accounting Standard 1 (IAS 1) is shown in Table 2.10. The format is flexible and not all companies will use the same format.

Using the examples above for Next plc, Table 2.11 shows that the balance sheet 'balances'.

Table 2.10 ABC plc balance sheet as at 31 December 2012

	2012 £m	2012 £m	2011 £m	2011 £m
Assets				
Non-current assets				
Property, plant and equipment	X		X	
Goodwill	X		X	
Other intangible assets	X		X	
Available for sale investments	X		X	
		X		X
Current assets				
Inventories	X		X	
Trade receivables	X		X	
Other current assets	X		X	
Cash and cash equivalents	X		X	
		X		X
Total assets		X		X
Equity and liabilities				
Share capital	X		X	
Other reserves	X		X	
Retained earnings	X		X	
Total equity		X		X
Non-current liabilities				
Long-term borrowings	X		X	
Deferred tax	X		X	
Long-term provisions	X		X	
Total non-current liabilities		X		X
Current liabilities				
Trade and other payables	X		X	
Short-term borrowings	X		X	
Current portion of long term borrowings	X		X	
Current tax payable	X		X	
Short-term provisions	X		X	
Total current liabilities		X		X
Total equity and liabilities		X		X

Table 2.11

At January 2012	£m	£m
Non-current assets	714.3	
Current assets	1,139.9	
Total assets		**1854.2**
Non-current liabilities	889.1	
Current liabilities	742.4	
Total liabilities	1,631.5	
Equity	222.7	
Total equity and liabilities		**1854.2**

2.5 Income and expenses

Income and expenses are portrayed in 'the income statement' (or trading and profit and loss account). The income statement is sometimes referred to as the 'financial history book' as it shows us what has happened over the past year. We do not add all the income and then take off all the expenses, although the net effect of doing that would be the same. We break it down into stages. For a retail company the stages might be as follows:

1   Revenue (sales or turnover) – cost of sales = gross profit.
2   Gross profit – company expenses and other income = trading profit.
3   Trading profit + or – results from investments = operating profit.
4   Operating profit – finance costs and income = profit before taxation.
5   Profit before taxation – taxation = profit for the year.

It is clear from that list that we should be very careful when using the word 'profit' to say which profit we are talking about.

Table 2.12 Next plc consolidated income statement for the financial year ended 28 January 2012

	2012 £m	2011 £m
Revenue	3,441.1	3,297.7
Cost of sales	(2,395.8)	(2,332.6)
Gross profit	1,045.3	965.1
Distribution costs	(245.7)	(223.2)
Administrative expenses	(201.3)	(179.1)
Other gains	2.0	2.2
Trading profit	600.3	565.0
Share of results of associates	1.5	1.8
Operating profit	601.8	566.8
Finance income	6.6	0.9
Finance costs	(28.9)	(24.3)
Profit before taxation	579.5	543.4
Taxation	145.3	(150.3)
Profit from discontinued operations	40.6	7.8
Profit for the year	474.8	400.9

2.5.1 Revenue

Revenue is the value of the total trading income of a company, which will usually be its sales for the year, but not all companies have 'sales' (for example, a bank), so we use the term 'revenue' to be consistent.

2.5.2 Cost of sales

Cost of sales includes all the costs directly related to the revenue. For a retailer, that will mean more than just the cost of the goods that have been sold; it will include other costs directly related to that revenue. Many companies now disclose in the notes to their financial statements how much of their cost of sale relates to inventory items. Table 2.13 shows a comparison of the supermarket chains Tesco, Sainsbury's and Morrisons. We see from the data that the proportion of inventory items included in cost of sales is almost the same for each company. This suggests that they all include the same other expenses within that category and have been consistent with that policy in recent years.

Table 2.13

		Cost of sales	Inventory expensed in cost of sales	Inventory expensed as a proportion of cost of sales
		£m	£m	%
Tesco plc	2012	59,278	48,910	83
	2011	55,330	45,529	82
	2010	52,303	42,504	81
	2009	49,713	40,779	82
J. Sainsbury plc	2012	21,083	17,000	81
	2011	19,942	16,053	80
	2010	18,882	15,192	80
	2009	17,875	14,490	81
Wm Morrison plc	2012	16,446	13,346	81
	2011	15,331	12,380	81
	2010	14,348	11,548	80
	2009	13,615	11,016	81

2.5.3 Trading profit

Trading profit is arrived at after deducting expenses that are divided into 'distribution costs' and 'administrative expenses', and then adding any other income. That is all that appears on the face of the income statement, but there is further disclosure in the notes to the financial statements where specific expenses are shown. A list of some of the common expenses that are disclosed in the notes is shown opposite, but there may be others. Companies comply with legislation and accounting standards, but will only disclose what they have to.

Expenses shown in the notes to the financial statements include:

* depreciation and amortization;
* leasing costs;
* foreign exchange gains and losses;
* auditors' remuneration;
* employee costs;
* directors' remuneration;
* gains and losses on the disposal of non-current assets.

2.5.4 Finance costs and income

Finance costs and income mostly relate to interest payable and receivable, but can also include the costs of raising finance.

2.5.5 Taxation

Sometimes companies refer to this in their financial statements as 'income tax' as it is the tax on their income. This is, again, to fit in with translation into other languages for global companies. We must not confuse this with the 'income tax' that individuals pay on their income in the UK. In the UK, companies pay 'corporation tax'.

The regulations for calculating the taxable profit of a company are not the same as the regulations for calculating the accounting profit. We should not, therefore, expect all companies to show tax charges in their income statements that are the same proportion of profit before tax. This is clearly seen in Table 2.14.

Table 2.14

Based on 2012 financial statements	Profit before tax (PBT) £m	Tax £m	Tax as % of PBT %
Marks & Spencer	658.0	168.4	25.6
Next	570.3	142.9	25.0
Tesco	3,835	879	22.9
Morrisons	947	257	27.1
Sainsbury's	799	201	25.2

2.5.6 Segmental reporting

Many companies are involved in different activities – e.g. Tesco retail groceries and are involved in banking. The income statement combines the income and expenses for all the activities. To aid the user in making comparisons, companies have to show in the notes to their financial statements, an analysis of each activity they are involved in and for each geographical market they trade in. This is known as 'segmental reporting'.

Companies have to show the revenue and profit that they achieve in each segment. An extract from the notes to the Tesco plc financial statements for 2012 is shown in Table 2.15.

Table 2.15

	UK	Asia	Rest of Europe	US	Tesco Bank
	£m	£m	£m	£m	£m
Revenue	42,798	10,828	9,866	630	1,044
Trading profit/(loss)	2,480	737	529	(153)	168
Trading profit margin	5.8%	6.8%	5.4%	(24.3%)	16.1%

2.6 Cash flow statements

There is a third financial statement along with the balance sheet and the income statement – the 'cash flow statement'. Making a profit will not ensure a healthy bank balance and it is often a lack of cash that leads to a company failing as they will be unable to pay their creditors. For this reason, it is important that a company reports on what has happened to its cash flow.

Thirty years ago, companies did not produce cash flow statements. As the information in a cash flow statement can be derived from the balance sheet and the income statement it was, perhaps, not considered necessary. An increase in the use of financial statements by a wide range of users and the importance of cash flow has led to the introduction of this additional statement.

Example 2.5

• A new company is started with £100,000 in capital from its owners.
• In the first month they buy a machine for £60,000 and pay for it in cash. The machine is expected to last for five years (sixty months).
• Raw materials are purchased for £30,000. These goods are paid for in cash as, like many new businesses, the company may be unable to get credit.
• Finished goods are manufactured, incurring further cash costs of £30,000 or labour and overheads.
• These goods are sold to trade customers on credit for £120,000.

The company income statement for this first month is shown in Table 2.16, and the company bank account is shown in Table 2.17. So, despite making a healthy profit of £59,000 in the first month, the company now has an overdraft of £20,000 at the bank. It is important that this difference between profit and cash flow is explained to users of financial statements.

Table 2.16	
	£000
Sales	120
Materials	(30)
Other expenses	(30)
Depreciation	(1)
Profit	**59**

Table 2.17	
	£000
Capital	100
Machine	(60)
Materials	(30)
Other expenses	(30)
Cash balance	**(20)**

There are different ways in which a cash flow statement can be prepared, but the most common approach is as follows:

- Start with the profit from the income statement before any interest and tax charges.
- The first adjustments are for any items included in that profit figure that do not affect cash at all. The most common example is depreciation – an expense that does not involve an outflow of cash.
- Then we adjust for the differences between the figures used to calculate profit and the actual cash flow – for example, we use total sales for the calculation of profit, but that figure is unlikely to be the same as the total cash received from customers when a company sells goods on credit. This is measured in the cash flow statement by considering the change in inventories, receivables and payables. An increase in inventories or receivables will cause an outflow of cash, whereas an increase in payables will lead to an inflow of cash. For example:

Sales for the year	£2,000m
Receivables at the start of the year	£300m
Total cash 'receivable'	£2,300m
Receivables at the end of the year	£500m
Therefore cash actually received	£1,800m

The difference in sales (used to calculate profit) and the cash received is £200m, which is the same as the increase in receivables (500m – 300m).

- We then consider interest paid and received and tax paid. These will not be the figures from the income statement. The tax due on the profits for the year will not be paid until the following year.
- The next stage is to consider 'investing activities'. This relates mainly to the acquisition and disposal of non-current assets. If a company buys a machine, there is no immediate effect on profit but a significant effect on cash flow.
- The final stage is to consider 'financing activities'. This relates to finance raised or repaid during the year. If a company issues shares or takes out a loan, there will be an inflow of cash but no effect on profit.

A simple cash flow statement can be produced using the figures from Example 2.5:

Profit for the year	£59,000
Add back the 'non-cash item' – depreciation	£1,000
Change in receivables (increase from 0)	(£120,000)
Net cash outflow from operations	(£60,000)
Investing activity – new machine	(£60,000)
Financing activity – capital introduced	(£100,000)
Net decrease in cash	(£20,000)

Table 2.5 shows that cash balances for Next plc rose from £49.3m in 2011 to £56.4m in 2012 – a rise of £7.1m. Bank overdrafts fell by £2.6m. Overall, they had £9.7m more cash at the end of the 2012 financial year than they had at the start (7.1 + 2.6 = 9.7). However, the income statement shows that the profit for the year after all expenses was £474.8m.

Table 2.18 shows information extracted from the cash flow statement of Next plc for the financial year ended in January 2012.

Table 2.18

	£m
Operating profit	**604.7**
Adjustments for 'non-cash' items	190.7
Increase in inventories	(3.6)
Increase in receivables	(93.8)
Increase in payables	(28.2)
Cash generated from operations	**669.8**
Tax paid	(143.9)
Net cash from operating activities	**525.9**
Net cash from investing activities	(70.2)
Net cash from financing activities	(446.1)
Net increase in cash	**9.6**

Table 2.18 shows what has happened to the cash balances. In this case, the cash has mostly been spent on new assets ('investing activities') and on repaying finance ('financing activities').

Problems

1 What would be the impact of the following transactions? (In each box you should state increase, decrease or no effect.)

	Cash flow	Profit	Assets	Liabilities	Equity
A sale on credit terms					
Buy machinery for cash					
Charge depreciation on machinery					
An issue of new shares					
Payment of a dividend to shareholders					
Sell a non-current asset for less than book value					
Make a payment to a credit supplier					
Receive cash from a credit customer					
Buy goods for resale on credit					
Repurchase shares for cash					

2 Do the following transactions involve capital or revenue expenditure?
   (a) A company buys a laptop computer for administrative use.
   (b) A motor vehicle is fitted with a new engine that will extend its useful life.
   (c) An advertising campaign costing £20m is launched with the aim of building the brand name of a company.
   (d) A football club pays £50m for a new player who signs a five-year contract.
   (e) A pharmaceutical company spends £30m researching a new drug.

Activity

Examine some annual reports for companies in a range of industries and observe the similarities and the differences.

Discussion topics

1 Do published balance sheets and the relevant notes to the balance sheet contain enough information for most users of financial statements? If not, what else should be published? (This topic will be revisited towards the end of the book.)
2 Should financial statements be adjusted to reflect current values rather than historic costs?

Chapter 3

Analysing profitability

3.1 Ratio analysis

The first two chapters have covered what the financial statements contain. Now we can start to analyse that data and hopefully draw some conclusions that would help a user of those financial statements to make some economic decisions.

The analysis will be split into distinct categories in the next four chapters:

- profitability;
- liquidity;
- gearing;
- shareholder interests (or 'investment ratios').

However, it is important that, when we analyse the financial statements of a company, we do not look at each of the above categories in isolation. For example, it is possible that a change in profitability (this chapter) has a direct impact on liquidity (to be covered in Chapter 4).

The key to good analysis is having valid comparisons for our results. There is always a need to compare the results obtained with both previous accounting periods and the results for other companies.

The process used to analyse company financial statements is often referred to as 'ratio analysis', although not all the calculations carried out are 'ratios'.

The profit, or 'bottom line' of a company is often the figure that users look for first. Before looking at the profitability ratios commonly used, we should ask the following questions about the profit shown in the financial statements.

- Is there a profit or a loss?
- Is it more or less than in previous years?
- Have any large or unusual transactions been included in the income statement this year that have neither arisen before nor are they likely to arise again in the future?
- What have been the relative changes in revenue, expenses and profit?

To aid the analysis of trends, most companies include a five-year summary of their results in their financial statements; this is usually found towards the end of that annual report. The following trends can be seen for Next plc over the last five years (Table 3.1):

Table 3.1

	2012	2011	2010	2009	2008
Revenue (£m)	3,441.1	3,297.7	3,406.5	3,271.5	3,329.1
% change from previous year	4.3%	−3.2%	4.1%	−1.7%	
Operating profit (£m)	600.3	565.0	529.8	478.3	537.1
% change from previous year	6.2%	6.6%	10.8%	−11.0%	
Profit before tax (£m)	570.3	543.4	505.3	428.8	498.1
% change from previous year	5.0%	7.5%	17.8%	−13.9%	
Profit for the year (£m)	474.8	400.9	364.0	302.3	353.9
% change from previous year	18.4%	10.1%	20.4%	−14.6%	

We can see that there have been steadily rising profits over this period despite the dip in 2009. Profits have risen proportionately more than revenues, suggesting that there have been some cost efficiencies. It is important to stress, however, that we cannot assume that because there have been steady increases in the past, these will continue into the future.

3.2 Return on capital employed

Return on capital employed (ROCE) is often used as a key indicator of the profitability of a company. It is often quoted by companies and referred to in the financial press. However, we must be very careful in using it as it is not always calculated in the same way and can sometimes be misleading.

ROCE measures the profitability of a company relative to the book value of the total funds invested in that company. It is a relative measure, and therefore enables us to compare companies of different sizes. A profit of £10m in Company A appears better than a profit of £1m in Company B. If £200m has been invested in Company A (ROCE = 5%) and £10m has been invested in Company B (ROCE = 10%) it would appear that Company B has used the funds invested more efficiently.

ROCE = (Profit/Capital employed) × 100 (%)

Unfortunately, there are no regulations that say which profit figure should be used or how we should measure capital employed. This could lead to two companies with identical results claiming different ROCE figures.

The most common approach is to use 'profit before interest and tax' (PBIT) as the numerator, and the total of a company's equity and debt (interest-bearing long-term borrowings) as the denominator. If Company C has £2m invested in it, all from its shareholders (equity), and Company D also has £2m invested but has £1m from a bank loan (debt) and £1m from shareholders (equity), only Company D will pay interest, so to compare their relative performance we should consider the profit before that interest.

A common alternative to using equity + debt for capital employed is to use the assets acquired by that capital instead. The measure used in this approach is total assets less current liabilities (TALCL). If all the non-current liabilities of a company relate to interest-bearing debt, then TALCL will be the same as equity + debt.

If ROCE is used in reporting performance, that report should always say how it has been calculated to avoid any confusion. Sometimes the approaches used by companies are very complex and although there may be good reasons for this, it does not aid comparisons. For example, Tesco plc define ROCE in their annual report in 2011 as: 'profit before interest after tax divided by the calculated average of net assets plus net debt plus dividend creditor less net assets held for resale'.

ROCE will be affected by the accounting policies adopted by a company. One example would be the way a company depreciates its non-current assets; two companies with the same asset but different approaches to depreciation will show different profits in their financial statements. There are many more examples of subjectivity in the calculation of profit.

Another problem with the calculation of ROCE is time. The profit in the income statement is in current terms (it is based on income and expenses over the last year) but the capital employed may have been introduced many years ago and the book value may not reflect current value. If we use TALCL as the denominator, this may fall over time due to depreciation of non-current assets, and this could lead to the situation shown in Table 3.2.

Table 3.2

	Year 1 £m	Year 2 £m	Year 3 £m	Year 4 £m
PBIT	90	84	75	60
Non-current assets at cost	1,000	1,000	1,000	1,000
Depreciation	200	400	600	800
Net book value	800	600	400	200
Current assets	150	150	150	150
Total assets	950	750	550	350
Current liabilities	(50)	(50)	(50)	(50)
TALCL	900	700	500	300
ROCE	10%	12%	15%	20%

The above example shows that a company can show improving ROCE despite falling profits. This may be an extreme example, but it is common to see high ROCE figures where companies have old assets that have not been revalued.

For Next plc, based on their recent financial statements, the calculation of ROCE is shown in Table 3.3.

Table 3.3

	2012 £m	2011 £m
Profit before tax	570.3	543.4
Interest (see note below)	25.2	22.5
PBIT	**595.5**	**565.9**
Equity	222.7	232.4
Debt	652.1	471.2
Capital employed	**874.8**	**703.6**
TALCL	**1,111.8**	**959.4**
ROCE based on capital employed	**68%**	**80%**
ROCE based on TALCL	**54%**	**59%**

Note: The income statement shows finance costs, but that is not necessarily just interest costs. For Next plc, there is only a small difference – the actual interest payable is shown in the notes to the financial statements – but for some companies the difference can be significant.

Interpretation

- The ROCE for Next plc is very high, so does that mean that they have been performing exceptionally well?
- They have done well, but perhaps not as well as the ROCE might suggest. The profits are in current terms and the book value of the debt is close to its current market value, but the book value of the equity is much lower than the current market value.
- The value for TALCL includes non-current assets, which are shown in the balance sheet at a value that is only 39 per cent of the original cost of those assets. The value above for TALCL is therefore also likely to be much lower than it would be if current values were used.
- The current market value of Next plc shares (in May 2012) gives a market value for the equity (also known as the 'market capitalization') of just under £5,000m. If this is used as the value for equity, the ROCE is only 11.8 per cent for 2012. This is probably a more realistic figure.
- The ratio has fallen slightly, suggesting that the increase in profits is not as great as the increase in capital employed. There has been a large issue of debt during the year and it may take time before there is a return on any new investments.

3.3 Return on equity

Return on equity (ROE) is a measure of the profit attributable to the shareholders relative to the book value of equity. For this 'ratio' we use the profit after all expenses and tax – the 'profit for the year' figure, which is sometimes referred to as 'profit after tax' or 'earnings'.

ROE = (Profit after tax/Equity) × 100 (%)

This measure has some of the same weaknesses as the ROCE, especially as it again compares a profit figure in current terms with the historic book value of equity. For Next plc, based on their recent financial statements, the calculation of ROE is shown in Table 3.4.

Table 3.4

	2012 £m	2011 £m
Profit after tax	474.8	400.9
Equity	222.7	232.4
ROE	213%	173%

As with the ROCE, the ROE is distorted by the very low book values of equity. A more realistic figure is obtained using the market value of equity – a ROE of 9 per cent (this is also known as the earnings yield and will be looked at again in Chapter 6).

3.4 Profit margins

A profit margin measures profit relative to sales. It tells us the proportion of sales that ends up as profit. We can also look at expense categories as a proportion of sales (expense margins) to help us to understand where there might be efficiencies, or inefficiencies.

Profit margin = (Profit/Sales) × 100 (%)

or

Expense margin = (Expenses/Sales) × 100 (%)

Profit margins can vary significantly between different industries. Some industries will traditionally have a high level of profit relative to sales; for example, a manufacturing company selling a relatively small number of high value items – like Rolls-Royce plc, who had a gross profit margin of 22 per cent in 2011. For other industries it can be quite small; for example, a retailer who sells a very large number of items at little more than cost price – like Tesco plc, who had a gross profit margin of only 8 per cent in 2011.

The 'norms' for industries can be useful to a wide range of users, but they are not widely available and are rarely provided free of charge. Organizations such as HM Revenue and Customs use them extensively to highlight anything unusual that might suggest a company is trying to evade tax.

Increases in margins can be due to operating efficiencies, charging higher selling prices for the same costs, or managing to reduce costs for the same selling price. They can also result from increases in volume, as Table 3.5 shows.

Table 3.5

	Year 1 £m	Margin %	Year 2 £m	Margin %
Sales	200		300	
Cost of sales	80	40	120	40
Gross profit	120	60	180	60
Expenses	100	50	100	33
Operating profit	20	10	80	27

The results in Table 3.5 show significantly increased sales. It is very likely that the gross profit margin will be at the same level because cost of sales will often vary directly with sales, especially in the retail industry. However, the expenses are quite likely to be fixed costs that do not increase as sales increase. Costs, like rent, utility bills and management costs will only increase if there is a significant expansion in a company.

The term 'operating gearing' is used to describe the proportion of the total costs of a company that are fixed. A high proportion usually suggests higher risk as those fixed costs have to be covered before the company makes any profit.

The data in Table 3.6 have been extracted from the financial statements of Next plc.

Table 3.6

	2012 £m	Margin %	2011 £m	Margin %
Sales	3,441		3,298	
Cost of sales	2,396	70	2,333	71
Gross profit	1,045	30	965	29
Expenses	443	13	398	12
Operating profit	602	17	567	17

Table 3.6 shows that the margins in Next plc have changed very little over the last two years.

3.5 Asset turnover

Asset turnover is a measure of how efficiently a company has used its assets to generate sales. We calculate the 'number of times' that the value of assets has been turned into sales:

Asset turnover = Sales/Assets (number of times)

A variety of different denominators are used. Possible approaches include using all assets or just non-current assets or TALCL or even capital employed. Again, we must take care when quoting figures to state which approach has been used.

Again, we get the problem of comparing current values for sales with the historic values of assets and this can again lead to misleading results, as shown in Table 3.7. The table shows that a company with the same assets and falling sales could have increasing asset turnover.

Table 3.7

	Year 1 £m	Year 2 £m	Year 3 £m	Year 4 £m
Sales	9,000	8,400	7,500	6,000
Non-current assets at cost	1,000	1,000	1,000	1,000
Depreciation	200	400	600	800
Net book value	800	600	400	200
Current assets	150	150	150	150
Total assets	950	750	550	350
Current liabilities	(50)	(50)	(50)	(50)
TALCL	900	700	500	300
Asset turnover	10 times	12 times	15 times	20 times

The data in Table 3.8 have been extracted from the financial statements of Next plc.

Table 3.8

	2012 £m	2011 £m
Sales	3,441	3,298
TALCL	1,112	959
Asset turnover	3.1 times	3.4 times

The asset turnover at Next plc has fallen over the last two years, showing that sales have not increased at the same rate as the increase in total assets less current liabilities. It is very difficult to say whether or not 3.1 times is a good figure without having information on other companies in the same industry. Any comparisons would also need to consider the average age of the non-current assets.

3.6 A useful link

ROCE is a key indicator, and it is a function of both the profit margin and asset turnover. If the profit margin or the asset turnover of a company increases, the ROCE will also increase.

$$\text{Profit margin} \times \text{Asset turnover} = (\text{PBIT/Sales}) \times (\text{Sales/TALCL})$$
$$= \text{PBIT/TALCL}$$
$$= \text{ROCE}$$

We can use this link to explain the reasons why the ROCE of a company may have either increased or declined. Companies can also use it in planning for the future:

- If a company was facing increased costs and was operating in a competitive market that meant they could not increase selling prices or volumes, then profit margins would fall. The only way, therefore, that the company could maintain or improve its ROCE would be to increase asset turnover by reducing the value of total assets less current liabilities.

Problems

1   Based on the data in the table below:

	This year £m	Last year £m
Revenue	2,400	2,000
Gross profit	720	600
Profit before tax	270	200
Profit after tax	150	130
Interest payable	10	5
Equity	400	360
Long-term borrowing	200	100
Non-current assets	500	480
Current assets	360	300
Current liabilities	240	200

(i)   Calculate the return on capital employed (ROCE).
(ii) Calculate the return on equity (ROE).
(iii) Calculate the profit margin for each of the profit figures.
(iv) Calculate the asset turnover.
(v)   Use parts (iii) and (iv) to check your answer to part (i).
(vi) Interpret the changes in profitability between last year and this year, clearly stating possible causes of those changes.

2   The financial statements of two companies in the same industry, and with the same financial year end, are shown below. You are required to analyse the profitability of each company and explain the possible causes of any differences between them.

Balance sheets

	ABC plc	DEF plc
	£000s	£000s
Non-current assets		
Property, plant and equipment		
– Cost	75,000	70,000
– Depreciation	30,000	57,000
– Net book value	45,000	13000
Current assets		
Inventory	2,000	900
Trade receivables	3,000	1,570
Cash	500	5,500
	–	2,470
Total assets	50,500	15470
Current liabilities		
Trade payables	2,000	1,440
Non-current liabilities		
Bank loans	10,000	10,000
Total liabilities	12,000	11,440
Net assets	38,500	4,030
Share capital	5,000	500
Share premium account	8,000	300
Retained earnings	25,500	3,230
Equity	38,500	4,030
Income statements		
Revenues	28,800	42,000
Cost of sales	16,880	21,050
Gross profit	11,920	20,950
Administrative expenses	(3,620)	(2,460)
Distribution costs	(5,760)	(4,620)
Finance costs (interest payable)	(1,160)	(1,120)
Profit before tax	1,380	12750
Tax	380	4,550
Profit after tax	1,000	8,200

Activity

Choose some companies and download their latest annual reports.

- Putting the following into any good search engine usually works – 'ABC plc annual report 2011'.
- It will help in later chapters if the companies you choose are quoted on a stock market as we will need to use the market prices of their shares.
- The financial statements of companies who are involved in retailing or manufacturing are usually easier to understand than those of service companies.
- Comparisons can be more meaningful if companies are in the same industry, but it can also be interesting to see the variation between companies in different sectors.

Calculate the ratios that are described in this chapter and try to draw some conclusions about the overall profitability of each company. Remember to use the information in the notes to the financial statements as well as the figures in the balance sheet, income statement and cash flow statement.

Discussion topics

1 Why do you think that, despite its flaws, ROCE is still seen as an important indicator of profitability?
2 How are the profitability ratios of a company useful to its employees?

Chapter 4

Analysing liquidity

The liquidity (or solvency) of an organization can be defined as its ability to pay its debts. However, that definition is far too vague; it is not just a matter of being able to pay debts, but to be able to pay them *when they fall due*. An organization may appear from its balance sheet to have insufficient resources to meet its liabilities, but that does not mean that it is insolvent.

Let us consider Mr Jones. Like many other individuals he has many debts. If he was required to repay them all next week he would have a problem, so does that make him insolvent? He might be able to pay his credit card, utility bills and so on, but would not be able to raise enough to pay off the mortgage on his house. But he does not have to. This is because his mortgage debt has many years before it has to be paid in full, so Mr Jones is probably not insolvent.

Measuring the liquidity of an organization from its financial statements is not straightforward. Reliable indicators of liquidity do not really exist. An indicator that points to low liquidity may suggest a problem, but could equally imply a high level of efficiency or increased profitability.

4.1 Working capital

The working capital of an organization is the money tied up in the short-term assets that may be (partially) offset by short-term liabilities. It is usually measured as the difference between current assets and current liabilities.

Working capital = Current assets – Current liabilities

Current assets includes inventory, receivables and cash. Current liabilities includes payables and short-term borrowing (e.g. bank overdrafts). The aim for most organizations is to be able to convert inventory into receivables (sales on credit to customers) and then receivables into cash in time to meet payments to payables (suppliers).

How much working capital should there be? There is no ideal figure, but generally a high figure suggests inefficiencies (this is because current assets are unlikely to be interest bearing) and a low figure can lead to liquidity problems. However, liquidity is never as simple as this, as there can be good reasons for a high figure and many organizations have negative working capital without facing insolvency.

4.2 The current ratio

Probably the most common measure of liquidity is the 'current ratio'. The current ratio of an organization is the ratio of its current assets to its current liabilities.

Current ratio = Current assets : Current liabilities

A company with £5m in current assets and £2m in current liabilities would therefore have a ratio of 5:2. This would always be simplified to 2.5:1 and is often simply stated as '2.5'. Therefore, the calculation is best remembered as:

Current ratio = Current assets/Current liabilities (:1)

Many people mistakenly believe that in order to be solvent an organization should have twice as much in current assets as current liabilities – a current ratio of 2. This would only be the case if the time taken to collect cash from customers is equal to the credit period taken from suppliers. A retailer who sells for cash but buys on credit can be in a strong liquidity position with a current ratio of less than 1. We can see this in the data in Table 4.1, based on the recent financial statements of Tesco plc.

Table 4.1

Tesco plc	At February 2012 £ millions	At February 2011 £ millions	At February 2010 £ millions	At February 2009 £ millions
Current assets	12,863	12,039	11,765	13,479
Current liabilities	19,249	17,731	16,015	17,595
Working capital	−6,386	−5,692	−4,250	−4,116
Current ratio (:1)	0.67	0.68	0.73	0.77

Here we have a very successful and efficient company with a low current ratio that has fallen over recent years and an increasingly negative working capital balance.

It is also important to state that an organization with a high current ratio may not be inefficient. Many manufacturers take a long time to convert their raw materials into finished production and therefore will legitimately have high levels of inventory.

We should also be aware of any seasonal factors that may distort the impression given by the current ratio. The balance sheet gives us the current assets and current liabilities for a company at the date chosen for the financial year end. However, the figures on that date may not be representative of the whole year.

Case study

The data in Table 4.2 have been extracted from the financial statements of a company. What is the current liquidity position of this company? (Remember to consider what may have caused the changes.)

Table 4.2

Last year	£m	This year	£m
Inventory	2	Inventory	1
Receivables	2	Receivables	1
Cash	1	Cash	0.5
Current assets	5	Current assets	2.5
Payables	2.5	Payables	5
Current ratio (:1)	2	Current ratio (:1)	0.5

Interpretation 1

The company may have improved efficiency in ordering and inventory control, and can now satisfy customers from a much lower inventory level. To generate cash, customers may have been offered a discount for the early settlement of what they owe. The cash generated may have been reinvested in new non-current assets. The company may be paying suppliers late deliberately and those suppliers accept this as they need the business and are, therefore, unlikely to charge interest. Overall, the company could be being more efficient this year and have new assets that could further improve that efficiency.

Interpretation 2

The company may have less inventory because suppliers who have not been paid will not supply them. Receivables may be down because there have been less sales and payables may have risen because of a shortage of cash. Overall, the company is having difficulties and may even be insolvent.

Which is the correct interpretation?

Based on the information given, we cannot say which of the two interpretations is nearer to the real situation. These are two extreme views and the real situation could be anywhere between them. To determine which is nearer to the truth we need more information. For example, if the company is showing improved profitability, we are likely to be closer to interpretation 1. To further our understanding of what has actually happened, we could read the Chairman's Statement and the Report of the Directors in the company's accounts.

With this in mind, we should never make rash judgements based only on current ratios alone. Looking at trends in current ratios does not really help either. Without further information a falling ratio can be a sign of improved efficiency or a sign of solvency problems. A rising ratio could be a sign of worsening efficiency or, on the other hand, could indicate a change of strategy to generate more profits (e.g. holding a wider range of products to generate more sales or offering better credit terms to customers). Any interpretation should be based on consistency and as such we should ask: 'Are the results consistent with the organization's strategy and the economic environment?'

4.3 The quick ratio

The quick ratio (sometimes referred to as the 'acid test' ratio) is similar to the current ratio but only considers those current assets that are 'quickly' turned into cash. Therefore, the calculation takes inventory away from current assets before comparing to current liabilities.

Quick ratio = (Current assets – Inventory)/Current liabilities (:1)

The same people who think that the current ratio should be 2 usually also think that the quick ratio should be 1. The logic of these people is that if an organization has as much in receivables and cash as it does in payables, it should be able to pay those payables as they fall due. Clearly, this still depends on the terms an organization trades under and a lower figure can again imply efficiency rather than a lack of liquidity, and a higher figure does not necessarily imply inefficiencies.

Consider a retail organization. We would expect most sales to be for cash, but purchases are likely to be made on credit and some payables will not be due in the very near future – for example, a profitable company will have a tax liability in its payables but this may not be due for payment for many months. Such a company is likely to have a quick ratio well below 1. Table 4.3 shows the quick ratio for Tesco plc.

Table 4.3

Tesco plc	At February 2012 £ millions	At February 2011 £ millions	At February 2010 £ millions	At February 2009 £ millions
Current assets – inventory	9,274	8,877	9,036	10,810
Current liabilities	19,249	17,731	16,015	17,595
Quick ratio (:1)	0.48	0.50	0.56	0.61

The above table shows how a company can be very successful and solvent with a low, and falling, quick ratio.

Case study

The data in Table 4.4 have been extracted from the financial statements of a company. What is the current liquidity position of this company? (Remember to consider what may have caused the changes.)

Table 4.4

Last year	£m	This year	£m
Inventory	2.5	Inventory	2.5
Receivables	2	Receivables	4.5
Cash	0.5	Cash	0
Current assets	5	Current assets	7
Payables	2.5	Payables	1.5
Quick ratio (:1)	1	Quick Ratio (:1)	3

Interpretation 1

The company may have become inefficient. Customers may be taking longer to settle their accounts – this can adversely affect liquidity and increase the potential for bad debts. The company may also be paying its suppliers more promptly and may not be taking full advantage of the credit available to them. In the longer term, this could lead to cash flow problems.

Interpretation 2

In order to compete, the company may be deliberately offering its customers more credit. This should increase sales and lead to increased profits. The company may be paying suppliers early to qualify for attractive cash (early settlement) discounts, which effectively make the goods that they buy cheaper and so should further increase profits.

Which is the correct interpretation?

Again, based on the information given, we cannot say which of the two interpretations is nearer to the real situation. These are two extreme views and the real situation could be anywhere between them. To determine which is nearer to the truth, again we need more information about the strategy of the company and the economic environment in which it operates.

4.4 Inventory

A large proportion of companies hold significant amounts of inventory (some will refer to it as stock). The key decision to make is how much inventory should be held. Hold too much and the company could be inefficient, but not holding enough could lead to lost sales and a damaged reputation.

The costs of holding inventory include:

- the space it occupies (rent etc.);
- insurance;
- theft;
- obsolescence (in 2011/12 Next plc had to reduce some inventory to a selling price that was below cost, costing them £79.4m);
- the cost of the capital used to finance the purchase of the inventory;
- staff costs.

The benefits of holding an inventory include:

- being able to satisfy more customers (bigger range of products);
- being able to satisfy customers more promptly;
- cheaper prices from buying in bulk;
- holding gains can be made in times of rising prices.

Companies who run out of an inventory item are said to suffer a 'stock-out'. Often the potential impact of stock-outs is a key factor in setting stock levels:

- No impact – the customer will return to buy the goods when they are next in stock.
- Minor impact – the loss of the profit on this sale (the customer purchases the product from a different supplier but will return to their regular supplier the next time that product is needed).
- Big impact – the loss of the profit on this and future sales (the customer purchases the product from a different supplier and does not return).
- Major impact – the loss of the profit on this and future sales and damage to the reputation (goodwill) of the company, which causes other customers to seek new suppliers.

4.4.1 Inventory turnover

Inventory turnover measures how quickly an organization turns its inventory into sales – either as a number of times per year or as the average time taken:

Inventory turnover = Cost of sales/Inventory (no. of times)

or

Inventory turnover = (Inventory/Cost of sales) × 365 (days taken)

There are problems with this measurement using figures taken from published financial statements.

Inventory

We need an average level of inventory over the year to compare to the annual cost of sales (cost of sales and not sales because inventory is valued at cost) but we only have year-end data in the published financial statements. The year-end data could be very different from the average due to seasonal factors; for instance, a retailer of children's toys will have significant inventory in November (ready for the Christmas period) but may have a much lower level of inventory in January. We need to take this into account when we interpret the results of inventory turnover calculations.

Cost of sales

We will usually include more than just the cost of inventory items – especially for a manufacturer where it will include manufacturing costs such as labour and overheads. Some companies, although unfortunately not all, do include in the notes to the financial statements the value of 'inventory included as an expense', which is the figure that we need. Table 4.5 shows a comparison of three companies in the same industry (supermarket chains). The data in Table 4.5 show that the proportion of inventory expense that is included in cost of sales is almost the same. Therefore, if the aim of our analysis is to compare companies in the same industry, it would not matter which measure (cost of sales or inventory expensed) was used.

Table 4.5

2012 financial statements	Tesco	Sainsbury's	Morrisons
Cost of sales (£m)	59,278	21,083	16,446
Inventory as an expense (£m)	48,910	17,000	13,346
Inventory expense/cost of sales	83%	81%	81%
Inventory (£m)	3,598	938	759
Inventory turnover (no. of times)	16	22	22
Inventory turnover (days) based on cost of sales	22	16	17
Inventory turnover (days) based on inventory as an expense	27	20	21

The results in Table 4.5 for inventory turnover suggest that Tesco plc is less efficient at turning over their inventory than two of their main competitors. However, great care should be taken that we are comparing like with like before making such an assertion.

- Tesco probably sell more 'non-grocery' items (e.g. white goods such as washing machines) than their competitors and those items will not sell as quickly as groceries such as bread and milk. This will increase the average inventory turnover period.
- Tesco have many supermarkets overseas. In 2011/12, 3 per cent of their sales were made outside of the UK. Goods that are in transit, by sea, to those overseas supermarkets will be included as part of their inventory. This will also increase the average inventory turnover period.

When we interpret financial statements we must have valid comparisons. It is not enough just to compare companies in the same industry because variations in ratios may be due to key differences between the companies, as we have seen above.

Industry norms are available – for example, jewellery stores turn over their inventory, on average, only once a year, whereas a petrol station turns over its inventory every week (fifty-two times a year). However, we must be careful when using industry norms. As described above, the fact that Tesco takes longer than their competitors to turn over its inventory is not necessarily a sign of inefficiency.

4.5 Receivables

Most businesses will try to encourage sales by giving its customers a period of credit before they have to pay for goods or services provided. The amount of credit given is usually common across industries, although the time that customers take to pay will not necessarily be in line with those terms. The amount shown in a balance sheet for receivables will represent the amount owed to the company at the balance sheet date, net of any bad or doubtful debts, that the company expects to collect within the next twelve months. Receivables were previously referred to (and still are, under UK GAAP) as 'debtors'.

Companies do not have to give credit to customers, but if they do not they may find it difficult to find customers (unless they have a product that no other company has or they are offering a very good deal on the price of that product). A company could, however, offer customers more credit than their competitors in order to generate more sales.

The benefits of offering more credit:

* more sales to existing customers;
* attracts new customers;
* increased sales may lead to cost efficiencies.

The costs of offering more credit:

* initial reduction in cash flow may cause solvency problems;
* increase in bad debts;
* increased administration costs.

4.5.1 Receivables – time taken to collect

Time taken to collect = Trade receivables/Credit sales × 365

This ratio will not be relevant to all organizations – only those who sell on credit. For most retail organizations there will be no need to consider it.

As with inventory turnover, this ratio also has some problems when using data from published financial statements.

Credit sales

Some businesses trade partly on credit terms and partly for cash; they may not state the proportion of each that is included in the sales ('revenue') figure in their income statement.

Tax (VAT)

Sales are shown in the financial statements of companies net of VAT, but the receivables figure will show the total amount owed by customers including VAT. This could give figures for the above calculation that are 20 per cent (the current rate of VAT in the UK) more than they actually are. As with inventory, seasonal factors could distort the year-end figures used.

Table 4.6, for Next plc, shows how data can be extracted from the notes to the financial statements to give an indicator of performance that could be of use to a potential user. Next plc are a retail organization, but also sell clothing on credit through their catalogue business – 'Next Directory'. In their financial statements they show in the notes the sales that relate to Next Directory.

Table 4.6

Next plc	2012	2011	2010	2009
Sales/revenue (£m)	3,441	3,298	3,407	3,272
Next Directory sales (£m)	1,089	936	873	816
Trade receivables (£m)	711	642	643	610
Average time to collect (days)	238	250	269	273

We can see from Table 4.6 that Next appear to be increasing the sales made to Directory customers and reducing the time it takes to collect payments from those customers, suggesting improved efficiency. Further information in the notes to the financial statements, shown in Table 4.7, gives users the amount included in receivables that the company regards as 'doubtful' – that is, the amount that they may never collect due to the customer being unable or unwilling to pay.

Table 4.7

Next plc	2012	2011	2010	2009
Trade receivables (£m)	711	642	643	610
Doubtful debts (£m)	114	109	123	117
Proportion that are doubtful (%)	16	17	19	19
Average time to collect all (days)	238	250	269	273
Average time to collect excluding doubtful debts (days)	200	208	217	221

The proportion of debts that are regarded as doubtful looks high but, in their financial statements, the company takes a very prudent approach to assessing what is doubtful and the actual default rates (actual amounts that are written off as not collectable) are much lower – 2.7 per cent in 2012. Doubtful debts are deducted from receivables to give a net figure for inclusion under current assets in the balance sheet, which could lead a user to understate the liquidity of this and other companies.

4.6 Payables

The figure shown in published financial statements under payables is included as part of current liabilities in the balance sheet and shows the amount that the company owed to its suppliers at its balance sheet date. These liabilities would need to be paid within the following twelve months. 'Payables' were previously (and still are, under UK GAAP) referred to as 'creditors'.

Trade payables are often considered to be a 'free' source of finance. If Company A sells goods to Company B on 30-day credit terms, they will expect Company B to pay for those goods in 30 days' time. If Company B does not pay after 30 days but takes 60 or 90 days to pay, they will indeed have had a free source of finance. This is because Company A is unlikely to charge interest as they will not wish to jeopardize future sales to that customer. For many companies taking as long as possible to pay their suppliers without upsetting them is clearly an objective. There can be, however, indirect costs associated with such a strategy:

- The company giving the credit will incur higher costs if customers do not pay on time – they are likely to pass these costs back to the customer through higher prices.
- The company taking the credit may miss out on potentially valuable cash discounts that are offered for early settlement. For example, should Company B, who has an overdraft at 8 per cent interest per annum, take 60 days to pay or pay in 7 days to

get a 2 per cent discount? The 2 per cent is to save 53 days (60 – 7), so is equivalent to an annual compound rate of nearly 15 per cent. Therefore, they should take the discount and pay early even if it extends their overdraft.

• If in the future the company taking the extra credit has an urgent requirement for extra goods, they may not receive them due to their poor payment record.

• Large organizations that try to exploit smaller suppliers can lose the goodwill of their customers. If a large retailer was taking an excessive amount of time to pay its suppliers, this could lead to them receiving 'bad press', and that may put off customers. The large supermarket chains in the UK are very conscious of this and endeavour to pay their suppliers more promptly than they used to.

In analysing payables and liquidity, we must consider the different categories (trade and non-trade) of payables. Some may be due for payment in a relatively short period of time (e.g. trade payables are often due in thirty days or less) whereas others may not be due for many months (e.g. corporation tax can be due as much as nine months after the balance sheet date). It is rarely done, but there is an argument for leaving longer term liabilities, like tax, out of the quick ratio for the same reasons that inventory is taken out.

4.6.1 Payables time taken to pay

Time taken to pay = Trade payables/Credit purchases × 365

This is an important ratio for anyone with an interest in how long it takes a company to pay its suppliers. As with other liquidity ratios we have to be very cautious interpreting the results given by this ratio. A high number of days could mean that the company is having difficulties making payments or that they are making efficient use of a free source of finance. Again, the ratio can be distorted by seasonal factors.

Unfortunately, companies do not disclose purchases in their published financial statements – it is common to use cost of sales as an approximation. Cost of sales, or cost of inventory expensed (see above) will be equal to purchases adjusted for any change in the level of inventory. We also have the same tax (VAT) problem as with receivables that is described above.

Table 4.8

Tesco plc	2012	2011	2010	2009
Inventory as an expense (£m)	48,910	45,942	42,504	40,779
Trade payables (£m)	5,971	5,782	5,084	4,748
Average time taken to pay (days)	45	46	44	42

The time taken to pay suppliers of Tesco (see Table 4.8) appears to be increasing, but not at a significant rate. Interestingly, we can see that they sell their goods in, on average, half of the time taken to pay for them.

It is unlikely that the closeness of the figures for the three competing supermarket chains, shown in Table 4.9, is a coincidence. This is a ratio that is widely quoted and, as a high number of days may show the company in a bad light to its customers, companies will be keen to avoid having a ratio that is much higher than their competitors.

Table 4.9

2012 Financial statements	Tesco	Sainsbury's	Morrisons
Inventory as an expense (£m)	48,910	17,000	13,346
Trade payables (£m)	5,971	1,903	1,409
Average time taken to pay (days)	45	41	39

4.7 Working capital cycle

The working capital (or cash operating) cycle of an organization measures how long it takes between paying its suppliers and receiving cash from its customers:

Working capital cycle =   Time goods spend in inventory +
Time taken to collect receivables –
Time taken to pay payables

There is no ideal period for the working capital cycle and it will vary from industry to industry. A manufacturer (who has to turn raw materials into work in progress and then finished goods before selling them) will obviously take longer than most retailers or service industries that hold no inventory. We must also be wary of trends. A falling working capital cycle period may be a sign of efficiency (less time to turn over inventory and collect receivables, and longer time taken to pay payables). However, it could also result from liquidity problems as a falling working capital ratio for an organization will also mean a falling current ratio.

4.8 Overtrading

Overtrading is a working capital problem that can lead to insolvency – through being too successful. A company that grows too quickly might not be able to find finance for its growing working capital needs. Rapid growth is not always a problem but it always needs to be managed well so that the required finance is planned for and put in place.

Example 4.1

A company has operated successfully with the following working capital:

	£m
Inventory	1
Receivables	1
Current assets	2
Payables	1
Working capital	1
Current ratio	2:1

The company then has a marketing campaign that is very successful – business rapidly doubles. If the company maintains the time taken to turn over inventory, collect receivables and pay payables, the current ratio will be maintained, but they will now need £2m in working capital.

	£m
Inventory	2
Receivables	2
Current assets	4
Payables	–2
Working capital	2
Current ratio	2:1

Unless this company has plans in place to raise the required extra £1m, it could face insolvency.

Common symptoms of overtrading are:

- a rapid increase in turnover/revenues;
- a rapid increase in current assets;
- inventory turnover falls;
- time taken to collect receivables grows;
- time taken to pay payables grows;
- cash balances fall;
- current and quick ratios fall;
- debt levels increase.

Having the above symptoms may mean that a company is overtrading, but there could be other reasons for the symptoms, so great care is needed in interpretation.

Problems

1   Based on the data in the table below:

	This year £m	Last year £m
Credit sales	240	200
Credit purchases	150	100
Cost of sales	120	100
Inventory	40	10
Trade receivables	20	25
Trade payables	15	25
Cash at bank	35	–
Bank overdraft	–	10

(a) Calculate the current ratio.
(b) Calculate the quick (acid test) ratio.
(c) Calculate the inventory turnover as a number of times.
(d) Calculate the inventory turnover in days.
(e) Calculate the inventory turnover in months.
(f) Calculate the time taken to collect receivables in days.
(g) Calculate the time taken to pay payables in days.
(h) Calculate the length of the working capital cycle in days.
(i) Interpret the changes in the liquidity position between last year and this year, clearly stating possible causes of those changes.

2   The data in the table below have been extracted from the published financial statements of two companies that are in the same industry sector and that prepare their financial statements to the same year-end date:

	ABC plc £m	XYZ plc £m
Revenue	480	240
Cost of sales	240	150
Receivables	80	20
Payables	80	50
Inventory	40	40
Cash and cash equivalents	–	40
Bank overdraft	40	–

You are required to calculate appropriate ratios for each company, stating clearly any assumptions that you make, and then interpret the differences between the two companies, giving possible reasons for those differences.

3   The ratios in the table below relate to four companies in different industry sectors but for the same accounting period.

	Company A	Company B	Company C	Company D
Current ratio	1.0	2.0	5.0	0.7
Quick ratio	0.5	1.0	1.0	0.6
Inventory turnover	20	30	180	2
Time to collect receivables	0	30	60	60
Time to pay payables	45	30	60	90

You are required to suggest, and justify, which industry sector each of the companies might belong to based on their liquidity ratios.

4   Based on the data shown below, has the company been overtrading?

Last year	£m	This year	£m
Non-current assets	160	Non-current assets	210
Inventory	60	Inventory	150
Receivables	64	Receivables	135
Cash	1	Cash	–
Current assets	125	Current assets	285
Bank overdraft	25	Bank overdraft	80
Payables	50	Payables	200
Current liabilities	75	Current liabilities	280
Net current assets	50	Net current assets	5
Net assets	210	Net assets	215
Share capital	10	Share capital	10
Retained earnings	200	Retained earnings	205
Equity	210	Equity	21
Sales	1,000	Sales	2,000
Gross profit	200	Gross profit	300
Net profit	50	Net profit	20

Activity

Using the financial statements that you started to analyse at the end of Chapter 3, calculate the ratios referred to in this chapter and try to reach a conclusion on the liquidity position of each organization. Your interpretation should not be limited to the liquidity ratios calculated but should also consider other information from the financial statements.

Discussion topics

1   Why is the current ratio not regarded as a good indicator for predicting the failure of a company?
2   In Chapter 1 we considered the wide range of user groups who may use company financial statements. Which of those groups will be concerned with the liquidity of a company and why?
3   Liquidity is seen as a short-term problem, but does it need a long-term solution?

Chapter 5

Analysing financial gearing

5.1 What is financial gearing?

Financial gearing, or leverage, is a measure of the proportion of the finance invested in a company that comes from external sources, commonly referred to as debt. Financial gearing is usually regarded as a key indicator of risk.

'Operating gearing' relates to the proportion of the costs of a company that are fixed. The impact of operating gearing was seen in Chapter 3 when considering the effect of increasing sales volume on the profit margin. Profits will fluctuate more, relative to volume, in a company with high fixed costs.

Risk is not necessarily a bad thing. We normally associate high risk with the potential for high returns, and a company that uses debt wisely can generate very good returns for its shareholders. We measure risk in terms of fluctuations. If a company has returns that fluctuate widely from year to year, it would be seen as being a risky investment.

Consider the following companies:

- 'Ungeared plc' has no debt. The £2m invested in this company has all come from its shareholders from a mixture of share capital and retained earnings. This is an all equity company.
- 'Geared plc' also has £2m invested in it. However, for this company only £1m has come from the shareholders (equity) and the other £1m has come from a bank loan on which the company has to pay 10 per cent interest (debt).

Now consider the following scenarios:

- If both companies generate a return before interest and tax of 10 per cent, and both pay tax at 30 per cent, we get the results shown in Table 5.1, which tell us that the return to shareholders is the same in both companies.
- If both companies generate a return before interest and tax of more than 10 per cent, there is a much bigger increase in the return to the shareholders in Geared plc. If we double the profit before interest and tax in both companies, we get twice the return on equity in Ungeared plc compared with three times the return in Geared plc. See Table 5.2.

Table 5.1

	Ungeared plc £000	Geared plc £000
Profit before interest and tax (10% of £2m)	200	200
Interest payable	0	100
Profit before tax	200	100
Tax (at 30%)	60	30
Profit after tax	140	70
Equity invested	2,000	1,000
Return on equity	**7%**	**7%**

Table 5.2

	Ungeared plc £000	Geared plc £000
Profit before interest and tax (20% of £2m)	400	400
Interest payable	0	100
Profit before tax	400	300
Tax (at 30%)	120	90
Profit after tax	280	210
Equity invested	2,000	1,000
Return on equity	**14%**	**21%**

We can see, in Table 5.2, that any return above the 10 per cent needed to pay the interest all goes to the shareholders. An increase in profits does not mean that the company pays more interest, that cost is fixed.

- If both companies generate a return before interest and tax of less than 10 per cent, there is a much bigger decrease in the return to the shareholders in Geared plc. If we halve the profit before interest and tax in both companies, we get half the return on equity in Ungeared plc compared with no return at all in Geared plc. See Table 5.3.

Table 5.3

	Ungeared plc £000	Geared plc £000
Profit before interest and tax (5% of £2m)	100	100
Interest payable	0	100
Profit before tax	100	0
Tax (at 30%)	30	0
Profit after tax	70	0
Equity invested	2,000	1,000
Return on equity	**3.5%**	**0%**

We can see in Table 5.3 that when profits are low, the fixed interest charge has a much bigger impact on the returns to the shareholders. A decrease in profits does not mean that the company pays less interest.

The above example shows how profits fluctuate much more in the company that has debt and hence we say that company has more risk. If each of the three outcomes was equally likely, then the returns to shareholders will vary less in the company with no debt.

5.2 How much debt should a company hold?

This is another of those questions to which the answer is 'it depends!' Companies generating steadily increasing profits with a return on capital, before interest and tax, that is greater than the rate of interest can usually service a high level of debt.

- In the above example, as soon as the PBIT (profit before interest and taxes) is above 10 per cent (the cost of the bank loan), the geared company outperforms the ungeared company.

Companies with falling or fluctuating profits will usually be expected to have lower levels of debt. The level of debt can also vary from industry to industry. The construction industry and the transport industry traditionally show high average levels of gearing. The service sector also has a high average but also has many companies with no debt at all.

Companies need to consider the weighted average cost of the funds that they raise. We call this average (weighted by market values, not the values shown in the financial statements) the 'weighted average cost of capital', or WACC. It is generally agreed that companies should try to minimize their WACC.

So what happens to the WACC if a company raises new debt finance? There are two effects:

- Debt always has a lower cost than equity. This is because those who provide the debt finance take less risk than shareholders – they usually take some form of security and can be paid even if the company makes losses. The interest on debt will also reduce taxable profits and will, therefore, reduce the tax payable, making the net cost of the debt even lower. The effect of having more of the cheaper source of finance must cause the average cost to fall.
- If there is more debt, there is more risk for the shareholders. There will be bigger fluctuations in their returns, as the example above shows. If there is more risk, the shareholders will expect a higher return to compensate for that extra risk, and this will cause the average cost of funds to rise.

There has been a lot of research into the net effect on the WACC of a company when it raises new debt finance, but few practical conclusions have come from that research. It is common for a company to try different levels of debt to see the effect on its WACC and, over time, the company will settle on an acceptable level. It is obviously very important for a company to have some idea of the overall impact of raising new finance whatever the source. In many sectors the better performing companies have the lowest gearing.

A general rule that many companies follow is to try to match the term of the finance they raise to the uses that the money raised will be put to. For example, a company buying a new building will use a long-term source of finance, just as an individual would when buying a house. The individual would not think of buying a house and paying for it with a credit card, and neither would a company use a short-term source of finance to finance a long-term asset. This is one of the reasons why the construction industry has high average levels of gearing. Companies in that sector tend to be involved with medium-term projects and most medium-term sources of finance are debt. Equity should normally be considered as a long-term source of finance.

5.3 Gearing ratios

There is no standard definition for measuring the 'gearing' of a company. Some of the commonly used approaches are shown below:

- Gearing is a percentage of long-term debt relative to equity.
- Gearing is a percentage of long-term debt relative to capital employed (which can also be defined in many different ways).
- Gearing is a percentage of all debt less cash balances ('net debt') relative to equity or capital employed.

Other methods use average values rather than year-end values or use market values rather than values from the financial statements. Having so many different approaches means that it is very important always to state how gearing has been calculated when quoting the ratio for a company. This is not always done in practice, and great care must be taken when considering the gearing for a company that is quoted in the financial press.

The data in Table 5.4 have been extracted from the financial statements for Tesco plc in 2012.

Table 5.4

	£m
Long-term debt	9,911
Equity	17,801
Capital employed (debt + equity)	27,712
Short-term debt	1,838
Cash and cash equivalents	2,305
Net debt (9,911 + 1,838 – 2,305)	9,444

These figures could give the following measures for 'gearing':

Long-term debt/Equity = 56%
Long-term debt/Capital employed = 36%
Net debt/Equity = 53%
Net debt/Capital employed = 34%

The current market capitalization of the equity of Tesco plc (June 2012) is £24.4bn – over £6bn more than the value shown in the financial statements. Using market values will usually give significantly lower measures for gearing.

5.4 What is a good percentage for gearing?

Based on 'debt/capital employed', it is often considered that anything over 50 per cent is a high level of gearing. This may be true in some circumstances, but it will not always be the case. A company can do very well with very high levels of gearing as long as it can generate enough profit to service that debt without adversely affecting the returns to shareholders. Hence, we should always consider the ability of a company to meet interest payments when considering how much debt it should hold.

5.5 Interest cover

To measure the ability of a company to meet interest payments we calculate 'interest cover'.

Interest cover = PBIT/Interest payable

Interest cover is usually quoted as a 'number of times', and the higher the result is, the more able that the company is to service its debt. An interest cover of two or less is seen as a problem as that would indicate that more than half of the profits earned would be going on interest payments, so that by the time tax is taken off, there is very little left for the shareholders. Most shareholders would like to see interest cover at a level of four times or higher. If a company can meet its interest payments more than four times out of profits before interest and tax, then, as long as those profits can be maintained, the current level of gearing is not a problem – even if it is more than 50 per cent, as stated above.

There is a similar situation faced by individuals. When an individual wants to buy a house, it is likely that he or she will need a mortgage (a loan secured on the property purchased). Most responsible lenders in the UK recommend not borrowing more than three times the gross salary of the borrower. This is linked to their ability to repay the debt.

- Consider Mr Turner, who earns £50,000 per year. He is seeking a mortgage of £150,000.
- After tax and other deductions, Mr Turner would receive a net salary in the UK of approximately £36,000.
- The annual repayments on a £150,000 mortgage spread over twenty-five years would be approximately £10,500 based on an interest rate of 5 per cent.
- The mortgage payments amount to approximately 30 per cent of Mr Turner's net pay and this would be seen as reasonable. His 'interest cover' is just under five times.
- If he took out a mortgage for £200,000 (four times his gross salary), the mortgage payments would be almost 40 per cent of his net pay. During the 'sub-prime' crisis, some lenders were lending more than six times gross salary; those borrowers were always going to struggle to meet their repayments.

In Table 5.5 we see what could be regarded as high levels of gearing. However, as the interest cover is also very high, it is clear that those levels of gearing are not a problem for Tesco plc.

Table 5.5

	Equity £m	Debt £m	PBIT £m	Interest payable £m	Capital employed £m	Gearing debt/cap. emp. %	Interest cover
2012	17,801	9,911	4,246	411	27,712	35.8	10.3 times
2011	16,623	9,689	4,106	465	26,312	36.8	8.8 times
2010	14,681	11,744	3,707	531	26,425	44.4	7.0 times
2009	12,906	12,391	3,317	400	25,297	49.0	8.3 times

A very different situation is seen in the annual report of the Eastman Kodak Company at 31 December 2010 (Table 5.6). This company filed for bankruptcy in the USA in January 2012.

Table 5.6

	Equity $m	Debt $m	Loss BIT $m	Interest payable $m	Capital employed $m	Gearing debt/cap. emp. %	Interest cover
2010	4,917	5,994	(336)	149	10,911	55	Negative
2009	5,987	6,002	(28)	119	11,989	50	Negative

In this table we see gearing that is not that much higher than that of Tesco plc, but a clear indication that they cannot service that level of debt without making profits.

It is not always possible to predict failure (we will look at this issue in depth in Chapter 7) from gearing and interest cover ratios. Table 5.7 shows data extracted from the annual report of Game Group plc in the UK for the financial year to 31 January 2011.

Table 5.7

	Equity £000	Debt £000	PBIT £000	Interest payable £000	Capital employed £000	Gearing debt/cap. emp. %	Interest cover No. of times
2011	326,994	15,559	28,850	5,745	342,553	5	5.0
2010	331,555	23,908	89,128	4,917	355,463	7	18.1

Table 5.7 shows that Game Group plc had very low gearing and a good level of interest cover in this annual report. Game Group plc went into administration in March 2012.

5.6 The cash flow ratio

Another way of assessing the ability of a company to meet its debt obligations is to consider the 'cash flow ratio'. The cash flow statement produced by companies tells us how much cash that company has generated from its operating activities. We can compare this cash generated to the total of all of the debts of that company. We take total debts as being the same as total liabilities for this ratio.

Cash flow ratio = Net annual cash inflow from operations/Total debts (%)

Once again, there is no ideal ratio, but the higher the cash flow ratio, the lower the risks faced by the company.

The cash flow ratios for the supermarket chains Tesco plc, J. Sainsbury plc and Wm Morrison Supermarkets plc in recent years can be seen in Table 5.8.

Table 5.8

	Cash inflow from operations (2012)	Total debts (2012)	2012 cash flow ratio	2011	2010	2009
	£m	£m	%	%	%	%
Tesco	4,408	32,980	13.4	13.9	15.1	12.1
Sainsbury's	1,067	6,711	15.9	14.3	17.1	16.2
Morrisons	928	4,462	20.8	24.1	19.3	21.3

All three companies generate enough cash to be able to meet those liabilities that need to be met. Some of the liabilities are very long term – for example, Tesco plc have some debt that is not due to be repaid until 2057.

Problems

1   Based on the data in the table below:

	This year £m	Last year £m
Long-term debt	560	480
Short-term debt	50	40
Cash balances/(overdraft)	(20)	20
Equity	600	550
Profit before tax	120	100
Interest payable	28	24
Total liabilities	840	800
Net cash inflow from operations	126	96

(a) Calculate the gearing ratio for each year using at least three different methods.
(b) Calculate the interest cover for each year.
(c) Calculate the approximate rate of interest on the debt in each year.
(d) What assumption are you making in part (c)?
(e) Calculate the cash flow ratio in each year.
(f) Interpret the changes in the financial gearing position between last year and this year, clearly stating possible causes of those changes.

2   What is the 'WACC' of a company? How will it change when a company issues some new shares?

3   Is financial gearing a good indicator of the risks faced by an investor in a company?

4   What are the differences between operating gearing and financial gearing?

Activity

Using the financial statements that you started to analyse at the end of Chapter 3, calculate the ratios referred to in this chapter and try to reach a conclusion on the financial gearing of each organization. Your interpretation should not be limited to the gearing ratios calculated, but should also consider other information from the financial statements and the ratios calculated in earlier chapters.

Discussion topics

1   One of the tables used in this chapter shows data for Game Group plc. The company entered administration in March 2012. They had very low gearing, so why did they not borrow more money to help them to continue?

2   Why can some companies survive with high levels of financial gearing yet others fail with low levels of financial gearing?

Chapter 6

Analysing shareholder interests

An investment is only a good investment if you buy it at the right price. Shareholders and potential shareholders will be interested in profitability, liquidity and gearing, but must always relate that interest to the market price of the shares. For example, the financial statements of a company show that it has been very profitable, appears to be efficient in terms of liquidity and appears low in risk in relation to financial gearing. Would this company be a sound investment for a potential shareholder? It is likely that the good results would already be reflected in a high share price, and that would limit the potential gains that could be made.

Shareholders get returns on their investments in two ways. They can receive income from the company in the form of 'dividends' and will also hope that the market value of their investment will grow to give a 'capital gain'. These two types of return are not mutually exclusive, but it is rare to get very high returns from both. If a company pays a high dividend out of the profits that it has made, there will not be much left for it to reinvest, and will therefore be lower prospects for growth.

A company that pays consistently high dividends will satisfy those investors seeking a regular income from their investments. Companies that pay no dividend or very low dividends may not be in difficulty as the profits may be being used to stimulate future growth, which could lead to capital gains from an increase in the share price.

6.1 Dividend policy

Some researchers have written that dividend policy should be irrelevant – it should not matter how investors get their return.

* If a shareholder seeking growth receives a high dividend from a company that does not reinvest anything, then that shareholder can use the income to buy more shares, giving the increase in the value of their investment that they were looking for.
* A shareholder has 1,000 shares bought for £2 each and expects 10 per cent growth. The company pays out all of the profit made giving a dividend of 20p per share and no growth is expected. This shareholder will receive £200 in dividends. This could be used to buy a further 100 shares. The shareholder now has an investment worth £2,200 (1,100 shares @ £2), giving growth of 10 per cent.
* If a shareholder seeking income receives no dividend because the company decides to reinvest any profits made, the market price of those shares is likely to rise. That

shareholder could sell some of their shares to realize the income needed while maintaining the value of their investment. This is referred to as 'manufacturing dividends'.

- A shareholder has 1,000 shares bought for £2 each and expects 10 per cent income. The company does not pay a dividend but reinvests all the profits made, leading to an increase in the share price to £2.20. This shareholder can sell 90 shares to create an income of £198 (90 × £2.20) or 9.9 per cent. The remaining 910 shares will now be worth £2,002 so the value of the investment has been maintained.
- The above examples appear to work for the investors, but they involve some crucial assumptions that do not apply in practice. The first example assumes that the share price will not be affected by the dividend decision and the second example assumes that the reinvestment will lead to an increase in the share price, even after shareholders start selling their shares. Both examples also ignore any transaction costs associated with buying and selling shares.

In practice, most companies have very stable dividend policies. If the shareholders are used to receiving high dividends, a change to that policy is likely to upset them and they may take their investment to another company where they can get the income that they need. Vodafone plc is a company that is well known for paying out high dividends and in 2011 the dividends paid amounted to over £4bn, more than the profit attributable to those equity shareholders for that year.

Likewise, if shareholders are seeking growth, they will not be impressed if all the profits made are paid out as dividends. In 2011, 122 out of the 500 companies listed on the S&P (Standard and Poor's) 500 Index in the US did not pay a dividend. Some of the companies not paying dividends are very large companies – the list includes Google, Apple and Amazon.

The policy of having a stable dividend policy is sometimes referred to as the 'clientele effect'. The management of a company should treat its shareholders as 'clients' and give them the type of return they are seeking. In practice, shareholders seem to invest in a company because of their dividend policy, not irrespective of it.

Table 6.1 below shows some practical examples of the dividend per share paid by UK quoted companies in recent years.

Table 6.1

	Next plc pence	Tesco plc pence	Marks & Spencer plc pence	Game Group plc pence	Wolseley plc pence
2007	49	9.64	18.3	2.93	117.5
2008	55	10.90	22.5	4.40	40.8
2009	55	11.96	17.8	5.50	0
2010	66	13.05	15.0	5.78	0
2011	78	14.46	17.0	5.78	45.0

We can see the following from Table 6.1:

- Next plc and Tesco plc have been able to maintain stable growth in the dividend per share paid to shareholders.
- The dividends policy adopted by Marks & Spencer plc reflects that of many other companies who paid lower dividends in 2009 and 2010 due to the recession in the economy.
- Game Group plc shows healthy growth in dividend per share but this was not an indicator of expected growth in the future as the company entered administration in 2012.
- Some companies, like Wolseley plc, have very erratic dividend policies.

The return received by a shareholder should be considered relative to the market price of the share. This ratio is known as the 'dividend yield'.

Dividend yield = Dividend per share/Market price of the share

Table 6.2 shows the current dividend yield for some of the companies referred to above.

Table 6.2

	Next plc	Tesco plc	Marks & Spencer plc
Dividend per share (2012)	90p	14.76p	17.0p
Market price per share at 16 May 2012	2,969p	318p	349p
Dividend yield	3.0%	4.6%	4.9%

The ability of a company to pay dividends out of the profits of that year is shown by the 'dividend cover' ratio. This gives us the number of times that the dividend could have been paid out of the profits attributable to the shareholders.

Dividend cover = Profit after tax/Total dividends for the year

or

= Earnings per share/Dividend per share

A low dividend cover means that a large proportion of profits made have been paid out as dividends. This could be a deliberate policy to give income to shareholders or because the profits were low for that year. A high dividend cover suggests that most of the profits have been reinvested for future growth.

Finding the dividends paid by a company in financial statements prepared under International Accounting Standards is not as straightforward as it was under UK GAAP. Under UK GAAP, dividends were shown as a deduction from profit after tax on the face of the profit and loss account. Under International Accounting Standards the dividends are shown as a 'change in equity', which is highlighted in a new statement appropriately called the 'Statement of Changes in Equity' (SOCIE).

Another recent change is that dividends are only shown in the financial statements if they are either paid or proposed in that financial year. Previously dividends were shown in the financial statements in the year that they related to even if declared after the end of the financial year.

Example 6.1

A company has a financial year ending on 31 March 2012 and declares the following dividends:

1   £2m on 31 May 2011. A final dividend relating to the profits made in the year to 31 March 2011.
2   £3m on 31 October 2011. An interim dividend for the year ending on 31 March 2012.
3   £4m on 31 May 2012. A final dividend relating to the profits made in the year to 31 March 2012.

Under UK GAAP the company would show £7m (items 2 and 3 above) as a deduction from profit after tax in its profit and loss account for the year ended 31 March 2012. Item 1 would have been accounted for in the year to 31 March 2011.

Under International Accounting Standards the company would show £5m (items 1 and 2) as a reduction of equity in the SOCIE.

6.2 Earnings per share (EPS)

EPS = Profit after tax ('earnings')/Number of shares issued

The calculation of EPS is not as straightforward as the formula above might suggest. This is because it is very rare for a company to have the same number of shares in issue for the whole of a financial year. This has led to the disclosure of two EPS figures:

- basic EPS;
- fully diluted EPS.

The 'basic EPS' is based on a weighted average number of shares in issue over the financial period.

The 'fully diluted EPS' includes other shares that may not have been issued yet. An example would arise where directors of a company hold share options that they have earned but not yet taken up. Share options give the holders the right, but not the obligation, to buy shares at a pre-determined (usually very favourable) price. This EPS is based on the maximum number of shares that could have been issued.

Table 6.3 shows the EPS figures that were disclosed in the financial statements of Next plc for 2012.

The calculation of basic and fully diluted EPS is beyond the scope of this text. Unless there has been a significant change in the number of shares in issue the calculation of EPS, based on the profit in the income statement and the number of shares shown in the notes to the financial statements, is likely to be similar to the basic EPS disclosed, as shown in Table 6.3 for Next in 2012.

Table 6.3

Profit for the year attributable to equity holders	£474.9m
Number of shares in issue at end of financial year	168,740,000
EPS (= 474,900/168,740)	281.4p
Basic EPS disclosed	282.6p
Fully diluted EPS disclosed	275.1p

Trends in EPS are seen as very important indicators of the performance of the investment made by a shareholder. Next plc has a primary financial objective (as stated in their annual report each year): 'to maximise sustainable growth in earnings per share'. They believe that this is the way that they can create value for their shareholders. Table 6.4 shows that they appear to be achieving that objective.

Table 6.4

Year	Basic EPS (p)
2004	93.9
2005	120.2
2006	127.4
2007	146.1
2008	168.7
2009	156.0
2010	188.5
2011	221.9
2012	282.6

Table 6.5

Year	Basic EPS (p)	Issued shares (m)
2004	93.9	265
2005	120.2	261
2006	127.4	246
2007	146.1	227
2008	168.7	201
2009	156.0	197
2010	188.5	191
2011	221.9	181
2012	282.6	169

However, we must not conclude from this table that the growth in EPS is all due to growth in profits made. Next plc have been able to show higher EPS figures year on year by reducing the number of shares in issue as well as by increasing profits. A company can buy back its own shares and then cancel them in order to reduce its share capital and many companies have done this in recent years.

Share buy-back schemes are usually used when a company does not expect to achieve the growth expected by shareholders. If profits of a company are expected to stagnate, that company can still increase EPS by reducing the number of shares in issue. The cost of the buy-back is met out of retained profits. We can see the effect for Next plc in Table 6.5.

6.3 The price earnings ratio

The price earnings (PE) ratio is a very important indicator. It is disclosed alongside the share price of a company in the listings shown in the financial press, and movements in it are watched closely by investors. It is a multiple of the number of times that EPS is covered by the current share price:

PE = Market price of a share/EPS

In theory, with certain assumptions made, PE can be thought of as a constant, meaning that an increase in EPS will result in an increase in the market price of a share:

2011 – A company discloses EPS of 20p and has a share price of £2.40, giving a
    PE ratio of 12 (240/20).
2012 – The company discloses an EPS of 30p. If nothing else changes, the PE ratio
    will still be 12, giving a market price per share of £3.60 (12 × 30p).

In practice, things are not as simple as that, but we do see increased market prices for companies with increased earnings. The share price at Next plc has risen by over 30 per cent over the year to 30 April 2012, which is partly due to the increases in their EPS.

The PE ratio shows how highly investors value the earnings that a company produces. A high PE ratio usually means that, as investors are prepared to pay a high price for the share relative to EPS, a high growth rate is expected. PE ratios tend to be similar for companies that are of the same size and are in the same industry, and therefore can reflect the growth expected from that industry.

Table 6.6 shows a range of PE ratios for companies in different sectors (these PE ratios relate to prices on 17 May 2012). The PE ratios shown do not seem to show a similarity within each sector. A high PE may be due to the most recently reported earnings being lower than normal and not typical of that company. Prices will always reflect expected future performance, whereas earnings relate to the past.

Table 6.6

Sector	Company	PE ratio
Banks	Barclays	7.4
	HSBC	15.4
	Santander	8.3
	Standard Chartered	10.5
Retailers	Dunelm	16.8
	Marks & Spencer	9.2
	Next	10.6
	Tesco	8.8
Media	BSkyB	12.3
	ITV	12.9
	Rightmove	33.3
	Trinity Mirror	1.1

6.4 Earnings yield

Another ratio that is often quoted is the 'earnings yield' of a share. This ratio gives us the total return relative to the market price of the share.

Earnings yield = EPS/Market price of a share (%)

We need to be careful when interpreting this ratio. A low earnings yield might suggest that the company is not performing very well relative to its share price, but this is not necessarily true. The earnings yield calculation is actually the inverse of the PE ratio. A low earnings yield of 4 per cent is the same as a PE ratio of 25. Hence, the low earnings yield is likely to be due to the high expectation of future growth rather than low current profitability. Earnings yield does give a more reliable indication of the current return being earned by shareholders than the 'return on equity' that we came across in Chapter 3.

The earnings yield for the same companies that we saw earlier is shown in Table 6.7.

Table 6.7

Sector	Company	Earnings yield %
Banks	Barclays	13.5
	HSBC	6.5
	Santander	12.0
	Standard Chartered	9.5
Retailers	Dunelm	6.0
	Marks & Spencer	10.9
	Next	9.4
	Tesco	11.4
Media	BSkyB	8.1
	ITV	7.8
	Rightmove	3.0
	Trinity Mirror	90.9

Problems

The table below shows some information relating to four companies in the same industry sector.

	Company A	Company B	Company C	Company D
Dividend per share (p)	10	0	100	5
Profit after tax (£m)	10	20	10	10
Number of shares issued (millions)	10	10	10	10
Market price per share (p)	150	225	130	140

1   Calculate the following for each company:

   (a) Dividend yield.
   (b) Dividend cover.
   (c) EPS.
   (d) PE ratio.
   (e) Earnings yield.

2   Describe the arguments for and against buying shares in each of the four companies. Which one would you invest in?

Activity

Using the financial statements that you started to analyse at the end of Chapter 3, calculate the ratios referred to in this chapter and try to reach a conclusion relating to the shareholder interests in each organization. Your interpretation should not be limited to the shareholder interest ratios calculated but should also consider other information from the financial statements and the ratios calculated in earlier chapters.

Discussion topics

1   Does the analysis in the activities carried out in the last four chapters enable a user of financial statements to make good economic decisions?
2   Why might a low earnings yield be regarded as a good indicator for investors?
3   Why might a high PE ratio not be good news for investors?

Chapter 7

Predicting corporate failure

Can the information included in the financial statements of companies be used to predict future success or failure? This is a question that has been the subject of much academic research. The research published does show some links between trends in certain ratios and company failure, but it is likely that the best research has not been published as it has been sold commercially.

The aim of the researchers has been to identify financial ratios that show significant differences between surviving and failing companies. It is commonly accepted that low profitability, poor liquidity and high gearing are important indicators of potential failure. What is needed, however, are quantifiable measures stating the levels that these financial indicators need to reach in order to indicate the future failure of the company.

7.1 William Beaver

William Beaver is regarded as a pioneer of research into corporate failure prediction models. In 1966 he published a paper[1] based on research that shows a link between failure of companies and a single financial ratio, sometimes referred to as a 'univariate' approach.

The 'Beaver failure ratio' is, interestingly, derived from information shown in the cash flow statement. Companies did not have to produce cash flow statements as part of their financial statements in 1966.

> Beaver failure ratio = Operating cash flow/Total debt

In calculating the Beaver failure ratio, total debt is taken to be the total of long- and short-term borrowings – those appearing under non-current and current liabilities in the balance sheet. Beaver's research showed that 70 per cent of firms with a failure ratio of less than 0.3 failed within five years. The research carried out by Beaver also identified the current ratio as a very poor indicator of future failure.

A calculation of the Beaver failure ratio for Game Group plc, a company that entered administration in 2012, is shown in Table 7.1. The calculations show that this company had a ratio close to Beaver's critical level of 0.3 in 2010, but a much higher ratio in 2011.

Table 7.1

	2011	2010
Short-term borrowing	£16m	£17m
Long-term borrowing	£15m	£24m
'Total debt'	£31m	£41m
Net cash from operating activities	£111m	£13m
Beaver failure ratio	3.58	0.32

Beaver's research was useful but has two key weaknesses:

* Company finances are very complex and varied, and it is unlikely that the status of all companies can be captured by a single ratio.
* The companies chosen by Beaver in his research had already failed, and hence his results may be sample-specific and not very useful for a predictive model.

7.2 Edward Altman

Edward Altman proposed a 'multivariate' approach, which he referred to as a 'Z score' in a paper[2] published in 1968. Having analysed different combinations of twenty-two different ratios, he concluded that a combination of five ratios had the best predictive ability. His original Z score equation was as follows:

$$Z = 0.012X1 + 0.014X2 + 0.033X3 + 0.006X4 + 0.999X5$$

Where:

* X1 = Working capital/Total assets: a measure of the liquidity of a company, companies in trouble usually experience shrinking liquidity.
* X2 = Retained earnings/Total assets: a measure of the cumulative profitability of a company relative to its overall size. Low retained earnings can be a result of low profitability and can result in a high level of gearing.
* X3 = Profit before interest and tax/Total assets: a measure of how productive a company is in terms of its earnings relative to its size.
* X4 = Market value of equity/Book value of debt: a measure that shows how close a company is to being technically insolvent (a value of less than 1 for this ratio).
* X5 = Sales/Total assets: a measure of how effectively a company uses its assets to generate sales.

For Next plc, based on the financial statements to 28 January 2012 and a market capitalization on 30 May 2012, the Z score calculation would be as shown in Table 7.2.

Table 7.2

	£m				
Current assets	1,140				
Current liabilities	742				
Working capital	398				
Total assets	1,854	XI =	21.5%	0.012XI =	0.258
Retained earnings	1,763	X2 =	95.1%	0.014X2 =	1.331
Profit before interest and tax	599	X3 =	32.3%	0.033X3 =	1.066
Market value of equity	4,970				
Book value of debt	652	X4 =	762.3%	0.006X4 =	4.574
Sales	3,441	X5 =	1.856	0.999X5 =	1.854
			times		
				Z score =	9.083

Altman's research suggests that a Z score of 3 or above suggests that a company is safe and a Z score of below 1.8 would suggest failure. Z scores between 1.8 and 3 were in a grey area, which suggests that, based on Altman's work, Next plc can be regarded as safe. An obvious problem with the Z score is that if a company has no debt, then X4 will be infinite and the conclusion would be that a company with no debt cannot fail.

Many researchers have followed up on the work done by Altman and many versions of Z scores now exist. Some of these are industry-specific or relate to the size of companies. As the Altman Z score requires a market value, it can only be used for quoted companies, so some researchers have developed versions that do not include a factor using market value. Some of the research considers some less obvious indicators as predictors of failure; a paper[3] by Peel, Peel and Pope published in 1985 considered a wide range of indicators, including the following:

- Director resignations as a proportion of the total number of directors.
- Director appointments as a proportion of the total number of directors.
- The change in directors' beneficial shareholdings.
- The time lag between a company's accounting year end and the date that the annual report was published.
- The change in the time lag in publishing accounts from one year to the next.

It would appear from this research that companies that change a lot of directors and are late in publishing their financial statements may be about to fail.

It is generally agreed that the financial ratios of failed companies can be seen, in retrospect, to have deteriorated significantly prior to failure. Therefore, we can use them to explain why a company has failed but, currently, no fully accepted model for predicting failure has been established.

7.3 Credit-rating companies

When an individual person applies for a loan or credit it is likely that the provider of the finance will carry out a credit check on that person. It is the same for companies.

There are organizations – for example, Moody's or Standard & Poor's – who will give an opinion as to the credit worthiness of companies.

These credit-rating companies do not publish how they calculate the credit rating of a company, but it is known that they look at a wide range of financial indicators, including the following:

- interest cover;
- free cash flow/total debt;
- ROCE;
- operating income/sales;
- long-term debt/capital employed;
- total debt/capital employed;
- inventories/cost of goods sold;
- quick ratio.

The list above only contains some of the indicators used, but does show that it is necessary to consider a range of indicators covering profitability, liquidity and gearing when assessing the credit-worthiness of a company.

7.4 John Argenti

The use of non-financial indicators based on non-accounting or qualitative variables is now being used extensively by managers of companies to measure performance. This is discussed further in Chapter 9. There has been research published that links failure to some of these qualitative factors.

A book by John Argenti,[4] published in 1976, suggests that a failing company follows a predictable sequence. First there will be 'defects', then 'mistakes' and then the 'symptoms' of failure become visible. Argenti divides defects into two categories: management weaknesses and accounting deficiencies.

Management weaknesses are:

- autocratic chief executive;
- the failure to separate the role of chairperson from that of chief executive, which is now seen as a standard requirement of good corporate governance;
- a passive board of directors;
- a lack of balance of skills in the management team;
- a weak finance director;
- a lack of 'in-depth' management;
- poor responsiveness to change.

Accounting deficiencies are:

- lack of budgetary control;
- no cash-flow plans;
- no costing system.

Argenti attributes a weighting to each defect and then awards a score for each. The higher the score, the greater the problem, and an overall score of 10 or less out of 45 is regarded as satisfactory.

If the management is weak, then this, according to Argenti, will lead to mistakes being made. He refers to three main mistakes that are likely to occur:

- gearing is allowed to get too high;
- overtrading occurs (see Chapter 4);
- the future of the company becomes dependent on the outcome of one big project.

Argenti weights these three mistakes equally and again attributes a score out of 45, with a score of 15 or less being satisfactory.

The final stage in Argenti's sequence is when the symptoms of failure become visible:

- Financial signs, according to Argenti, are not likely to appear until two years before symptoms of failure are visible.
- Creative accountancy may hide the financial signs. Sometimes failing companies issue optimistic statements that may include, for example, higher values for inventory and lower values for depreciation to boost profits. These changes may be difficult to identify by an outsider and may be the reason for some companies appearing to fail very rapidly.
- Non-financial signs, including frozen management salaries, delayed capital expenditure, falling market share and rising staff turnover.
- Terminal signs. At the end, the financial and non-financial signs will become very obvious even to casual observers.

Argenti attributes a score out of 10 to these symptoms of failure. Overall, Argenti attributes 100 marks (45 + 45 + 10) to give a total score, the 'A score', for a company. The lower the score, the better for the company. A score of 18 or less usually means that a company is not at risk. The companies at risk usually have scores in excess of 25.

Problems

1   Based on the data in the table below, calculate the Beaver failure ratio for each company and state which, if any, are potentially failing companies.

	Company A £m	Company B £m	Company C £m	Company D £m
Short-term borrowing	10	0	210	500
Long-term borrowing	200	420	0	5,000
Net cash from operating activities	70	140	70	3,000

2   Based on the data in the table below, calculate the Altman Z score for each company and state which, if any, are potentially failing companies.

	Company W £m	Company X £m	Company Y £m	Company Z £m
Current assets	100	56	200	400
Current liabilities	56	100	200	400
Total assets	400	200	600	1,000
Retained earnings	4,000	2,000	1,000	4,000
Profit before interest and tax	56	12	60	−60
Market value of equity	6,000	4,000	2,000	6,000
Book value of debt	1,000	0	1,000	2,000
Sales	2,000	1,000	1,000	4,000

Activity

For the companies that you have analysed in the previous chapters, calculate the Beaver failure ratio and Altman's Z score, and interpret your results.

Discussion topics

1   Should companies disclose their Z score in their financial statements?
2   Could a company with no debt ever fail?
3   Can an 'A' score be determined from information disclosed in the published financial statements of a company?
4   What else could be disclosed in the financial statements of a company to enable users to predict potential failure? Should companies be made to disclose that information?

Notes

1   Beaver, W. (1966) 'Financial Ratios as Predictors of Failure'. *Journal of Accounting Research*, Supplement 4.
2   Altman, E. (1968) 'Financial Ratios, Discriminant Analysis and the Prediction of Corporate Bankruptcy'. *Journal of Finance*: 189–209.
3   Peel, M.J., D.A. Peel and P.F Pope (1986) 'Predicting Corporate Failure – Some Results for the UK Corporate Sector'. *International Journal of Management Science*, vol. 14, no. 1.
4   Argenti, J. 1976. *Corporate Collapse: The Causes and Symptoms*. London: McGraw-Hill.

Chapter 8

Using other information in company annual reports

In the preceding chapters, the data used have been, mostly, taken from the three main financial statements: the income statement, the statement of financial position (balance sheet) and the cash flow statement. It is important that any analysis is not limited to what is included in these statements, but also to consider the notes that support them and other disclosures in the annual reports of companies.

Most companies can fit each of the three statements referred to above on to one page of the annual report, but the supporting notes can easily amount to sixty or more further pages. The notes to the financial statements are where all the disclosure requirements are met for items that do not have to fit on to the face of the three statements. This chapter starts by looking at what is disclosed on the face of the three statements and what is disclosed (some might say 'hidden away') in the notes.

8.1 Accounting policies

The first 'note' to the financial statements is usually a list of the accounting policies that have been applied in preparing them. These commonly include the following:

- Confirmation the financial statements have been prepared in accordance with International Financial Reporting Standards (IFRS) and with the latest legislation (for companies reporting in the UK in 2012 that was the Companies Act of 2006).
- Treatment of intangible assets such as goodwill. It is normal not to amortize goodwill, but other non-current assets will be written off over their useful lives. The estimates used for the useful lives will be disclosed here.
- The useful life of each class of tangible non-current asset is also given, but the policy is not usually very specific. The information for Next plc for 2012 is shown in Table 8.1.
- The method used to value investments, inventories, receivables and financial assets.
- A definition of what is included under the heading of 'cash and cash equivalents'.
- That revenues are shown net of any returns, and net of value added and other sales taxes.
- A description of how transactions involving foreign currency have been translated into sterling.
- A statement as to how the company has treated any leases, in particular the differentiation between finance and operating leases.

- The approach to the recognition of any provisions.
- The impact of any changes in accounting standards since the last annual report.

Table 8.1

Freehold and long leasehold property	50 years
Plant machinery and building works	10–25 years
Fixtures and fittings	6–15 years
Vehicles, IT and other assets	2–6 years
Leasehold improvements	The period of the lease, or useful life if shorter

8.2 Revenue

The income statement gives us one figure for the total revenue (for most companies this will be their total sales). The notes to the accounts give us more detail, although not as much as we might like. A company will give the revenue for each segment of its business by type of business and by geographical region. The segments are often vague – for example, Marks & Spencer simply split sales between UK and international, and their UK sales are split between 'food' and 'general merchandise'; there is no breakdown of general merchandise into clothing, furniture, financial services and other products.

If we are unable to see a detailed breakdown by specific segments, it becomes very difficult to compare companies as it is not known whether we are comparing like with like. If I wanted to compare grocery sales in Tesco and Sainsbury's in the UK, could I do that?

Table 8.2

	UK sales in financial year ending in 2012 £m
Tesco plc	42,798
J. Sainsbury plc	22,294

Are the two sales figures in Table 8.2 comparable? A user of the financial statements would probably treat them as comparable, but there are some key differences. For both companies the figure represents the sales of goods in the UK from retailing activities, but they do not sell the same range of products. Tesco plc, for instance, has a chain of garden centres ('Dobbies') and the sales from those stores are included in the above figures, whereas J. Sainsbury plc does not own any garden centres.

8.3 Costs

On the face of the income statement, the costs incurred by a company are divided into four general headings:

- Cost of sales
- Administrative expenses
- Distribution costs
- Finance costs

No indication is disclosed as to which costs appear under which classification. However, more detail is found in the notes in relation to some specific expenses that have to be disclosed. Some of the costs that have to be disclosed are:

- audit fees;
- directors' remuneration;
- staff costs;
- depreciation;
- amortization;
- gain/(loss) on disposal of non-current assets;
- leasing costs.

8.4 Profit

Profits, like revenues, must be shown for each segment of a company.

8.5 Taxation

The note to the taxation charge in the income statement will help to explain why the charge is not simply the profit multiplied by the tax rate. The tax charge for the current financial year will be adjusted for under- or over-provisions in previous years and will show any tax that has been deferred to future years. This is useful when trying to forecast future earnings.

8.6 Non-current assets

On the face of a company balance sheet, all that is disclosed is the total net book value of tangible and intangible non-current assets. The data in Table 8.3 are fictitious, but show the type of information that might be disclosed in the notes for property, plant and equipment.

From Table 8.3 we can make the following interpretations:

- The growth in the total net book value is mostly due to increases in land and buildings from acquisitions and revaluations.
- The land and buildings have had, on average, only 10 per cent (282/2,820) of their useful lives, and are therefore relatively new.
- The fixtures, fittings and equipment have had, on average, 75 per cent (3,510/4,680) of their useful lives, and are therefore getting quite old. This may imply a need for

Table 8.3

	Land and buildings £m	Fixtures, fittings and equipment £m	Total £m
Cost at start of year	2,400	4,560	6,960
Additions at cost	200	240	440
Revaluations	260		260
Cost of disposals	(40)	(120)	(160)
Cost at end of year	2,820	4,680	7,500
Accumulated depreciation at start of year	228	3,150	3,378
Charge for the year	56	470	526
Depreciation on disposals	(2)	(110)	(112)
Accumulated depreciation at end of year	282	3,510	3,792
Net book value at start of year	2,172	1,410	3,582
Net book value at end of year	2,538	1,170	3,708

significant investment to replace older assets in the near future, which may reduce the potential for the company to grow. It could also put a strain on cash flow in the future.

The same type of disclosure is also made for intangible non-current assets.

In recent years, a further adjustment has been introduced to financial statements that impacts on non-current assets. This new adjustment is 'impairment'. Impairment might arise if an asset is damaged or if it is no longer used in the same way. The value for non-current assets that is used in the financial statements should be the lower of:

• its carrying value in the balance sheet (cost less accumulated depreciation); or
• its 'recoverable amount'.

The 'recoverable amount' is the higher of:

• the fair value of that asset less the costs incurred in selling it; or
• its value in use.

If the recoverable amount falls below the carrying value, the asset has been 'impaired' and the value shown in the financial statements must be reduced.

Example 8.1

John plc has used a tangible non-current asset for the last four years. The asset has an estimated useful life of ten years and originally cost £10m. The company has received an offer of £4m for the asset and the buying company will cover all the costs of transferring the asset. The present value of the future cash flows from the continued use of the asset is estimated at £3m.

- The carrying value is the net book value. Based on straight line depreciation with no residual value, we get a carrying value of £10m – (4/10 × £10m) = £6m.
- The fair value less costs to sell is £4m.
- The value in use is £3m.
- This gives us a recoverable amount of £4m (higher of £4m and £3m).
- As this is less than the carrying amount (£6m), the value of the asset must be reduced by £2m and this reduction would be referred to as impairment.

If a company has significant impairment charges in any particular financial period, this can be seen as a sign that the company may be having problems. Indicators of impairment include:

- Large decreases in the market value of assets.
- A significant change in the technological market or economic environment of the business in which the assets are employed.
- An increase in the returns required by shareholders and debt providers as this will increase the company cost of capital. A higher cost of capital will give lower present values for future cash flows and hence lower, in use, values for assets.
- The book value of net assets from the balance sheet is greater than the market capitalization of the company. This would suggest that the book values of assets are too high.

8.7 Inventory

The notes to the accounts will give some details relating to the types of inventory held. Inventory will be split between:

- raw materials;
- work in progress;
- finished goods.

All types are shown at a value that is the lower of cost and net realizable value as defined in Chapter 2. No further details relating to the type of goods included in the inventory are disclosed; a company does not have to disclose what goods are included under each of the three types referred to above.

The inventory items that have been used or sold in an accounting period will be included in the cost of sales in the income statement. Most companies now disclose the amount of inventory that has been included in this expense category either with other costs (see Section 8.3 on page 77) or in the note for inventory.

8.8 Trade and other receivables

'Trade and other receivables' is usually given as one figure in the balance sheet. The notes break this down into:

- Trade receivables, usually shown in total and then after any allowance for doubtful debts. This often is an indicator of how efficient the company is in collecting debts from customers. A significant increase in bad and doubtful debts can also indicate problems in an industry as was seen in the financial statements of banks following the recent crisis.
- Any amounts due to the company from its associates will be shown separately in the notes.
- The only other common categories here are 'other receivables' and 'prepayments'.

8.9 Cash and cash equivalents

The note to this balance will show cash held at the bank or in hand, any amounts held on deposit in the short term and any short-term investments.

8.10 Borrowings

Borrowings will be split into current and non-current liabilities. Borrowings are current if they are repayable within twelve months. Overdrafts are usually repayable on demand and are therefore always current liabilities.

Example 8.2

If a company borrows £10m from a bank and will pay the capital back in equal instalments over the next ten years, £1m will be shown as a current liability and £9m will be shown as a non-current liability. The following year there will still be a £1m current liability but the non-current liability will be £8m.

Some companies use the markets to issue their own debt. Table 8.4 shows data extracted from the annual report of Tesco plc for 2012. The information in the table can give a user of those financial statements some useful information:

- Tesco plc are raising funds in several currencies, which can be a good way to reduce risks caused by fluctuations in exchange rates.
- There are a wide range of maturity dates. Companies usually try to match the maturity of debt to the life of projects financed by that debt. This suggests that Tesco plc have been investing in both long- and short-term projects.
- The difference between the par and actual market values of the debt give us an indication of the overall credit rating of a company. Using the data, we can calculate the yield to maturity implied in debt and this yield represents the return required by lenders. The lower the yield the better the credit rating for the company. Taking the £279m of 5.2 per cent debt repayable in 2057 with a market value of £274m, there is an implied yield to maturity of 5.1 per cent.

Table 8.4

	Par value	Maturity year	£m
2% USD bond	$500m	2014	317
5% MTN	£600m	2014	619
5.125% MTN	€600m	2015	526
4% RPI MTN	£282m	2016	288
5.875% MTN	€1,039m	2016	1,042
2.7% USD bond	$500m	2017	318
5.5% USD bond	$850m	2017	659
5.2% Tesco retail bond	£125m	2018	138
3.375% MTN	€750m	2018	638
5.5% MTN	£350m	2019	352
1% RPI Tesco retail bond	£60m	2019	59
6.125% MTN	£900m	2022	892
5% MTN	£515m	2023	401
3.322% LPI MTN	£287m	2025	290
6% MTN	£200m	2029	251
5.5% MTN	£200m	2033	249
1.982% RPI MTN	£240m	2036	242
6.15% USD bond	$1,150m	2037	897
5% MTN	£173m	2042	174
5.125% MTN	€600m	2047	635
5.2% MTN	£279m	2057	274
Other MTNs			162
Other loans			354
Finance leases			134
			9,911

Note: LPI = limited price inflation; MTN = medium-term note; RPI = retail price index; USD = US dollar.

8.11 Trade and other payables

'Trade and other payables' is usually given as one figure in the balance sheet. The notes break this down into:

- Trade payables usually relates to the amounts owed to suppliers for goods used directly in the trade of the company. Suppliers, and potential suppliers, will look at this figure to estimate how quickly they are likely to get paid.
- Any amounts due from the company to its associates will be shown separately in the notes.
- The only other common categories here are: taxation, other payables and accruals.

8.12 Share capital

The note to the share capital figure will show the number of shares that a company is authorized to issue and the number already issued. The note also shows any movements in the number of shares in issue from one year to the next. This note is useful because it gives an indication of the ability of a company to raise equity finance from an issue of new shares. Companies can increase their authorized share capital with the support of existing shareholders and, if this has happened, it is a very good sign of a future share issue.

Other changes in equity will be highlighted in the Statement of Changes in Equity (SOCIE).

8.13 Other disclosure

There are some items of information that have to be disclosed in the notes to the financial statements that do not affect the income statement, balance sheet or cash flow statement.

8.13.1 Contingent liabilities

Contingent liabilities were defined in Chapter 2 as liabilities that will depend on a future event such as a legal case.

Example 8.3

A customer is taking an action for damages of £5m against Peter plc. When preparing the financial statements the accounting staff at Peter plc do not know the result of this legal case. They will need to seek professional advice.

- If the advice is that the customer is likely to be successful with their claim, then the £5m will be included in current liabilities.
- If the advice is that it is possible that the customer will be successful but not very likely, then no liability is shown but a note describing the potential impact is included.

8.13.2 Post balance sheet events

Post balance sheet events are events that occur between the date of the balance sheet and the date that the financial statements are published. There are two types of 'event':

- 'Adjusting events' will result in the financial statements being adjusted and relate to events that give new information relating to a condition that already existed at the date of the balance sheet.
- 'Non-adjusting events' will not affect the financial statements but may be important to users so their impact will be described in the notes.

Example 8.4

Rachel plc has a financial year end of 31 March 2012 and they expect to publish their annual report on 31 May of that year. On 15 April a major customer who owed £12m went into liquidation and it is considered unlikely that any of that debt will be recovered. On 30 April a fire destroyed a warehouse owned by the company and although the building was insured, the contents (an inventory that cost £5m) were not. How should these events be accounted for?

- The liquidation of the customer would be treated as an adjusting event and the debt would be written off, reducing receivables and increasing the expense of bad debts by £12m. This is an adjusting event because it is likely that the debt was not recoverable at 31 March and the news of the liquidation confirmed this.
- The loss of £5m resulting from the fire would not affect the financial statements as on 31 March; the inventory was unaffected. As this event is likely to have a material effect on the financial statements to 31 March 2013, details of it will be shown in the notes to the financial statements in the 2012 annual report.

8.14 The Chairman's Statement

The chairperson of the board of directors of a company always includes a statement in the annual report. This statement is rarely more than one page long and simply gives an overview of the performance and position of the company and refers to any changes to the members of the board (Chapter 7 describes some research linking changes in directors to potential failure). The chairperson will usually thank the staff for their efforts and refer briefly to the overall strategy of the company going forward.

8.15 The Directors' Report

All annual reports also contain a 'Directors' Report'. The common sections that are found in most reports are as follows:

- Chief Executive's Review – a more extensive review of the current financial performance and financial position than is included in the Chairman's Statement.
- A list of the principal activities of the company. This can help to explain why some companies that are apparently in the same industry have differences in their financial ratios.
- An overview of the strategies and objectives for the company. This may be important to a wide range of users, especially if there are to be significant changes.
- The outlook and priorities of the company are also covered in this report.
- Many companies include key performance indicators in their Directors' Report. Care must be taken when comparing these ratios for different companies because all companies may use different approaches to calculate the same ratios.
- The directors will refer to the key risks and uncertainties that they expect to face in the coming years.
- The directors will also report on what they are doing for their employees covering such topics as:

  - equal opportunities;
  - training and development;
  - employee share ownership schemes;
  - pension provision.

- A more recent addition to most Directors' Reports is a section on social and environmental matters. They will comment on ethical issues and their corporate responsibilities. Reports often comment on energy use, emission levels and reductions in waste. This section may also refer to the company's relationships with suppliers and customers, as well as health and safety issues.

- The directors have to disclose in great depth how they have been remunerated. All salaries, bonuses and share dealings are clearly disclosed for each director.
- The directors will also produce an extended section in their report on corporate governance issues and how they have fulfilled their obligations in respect of those issues.

Problems

1   The following measures relate to a non-current asset. Which value should be used in the financial statements?

(a) Net book value £20,000.
(b) Net realizable value £18,000.
(c) Value in use £22,000.
(d) Replacement cost £50,000.

2   Kate Ltd purchased equipment on 1 April 2008 for £100,000. The equipment was depreciated using the reducing balance method at 25 per cent per year. At 31 March 2012 the recoverable amount was £28,000. What, if any, further action is required?

3   A business has the following book values of its assets:

	£m
Building	20
Plant and equipment	10
Goodwill	5
Current assets	10
	45

Following a downturn in the market, an impairment review has taken place and the recoverable amount of the business is estimated to be £25m. How would the assets be valued in the balance sheet?

Activities

1   Go through the notes to the financial statements for the companies that you have analysed in the previous chapters. Do they help to explain some of the ratios calculated?
2   Does the review given in the Directors' Reports for the companies analysed agree with your analysis?

Discussion topics

1   Is there too much information in a set of financial statements making them hard to understand for many users?
2   The annual report for Tesco plc for 2012 includes 65 pages of 'financial statements' but only 5 of those pages relate to the actual statements and the rest of the pages are for the notes. Why is there so much information in the notes and so little in the statements themselves?
3   What other information could be given in the notes to help users to make economic decisions?

Chapter 9

Business valuations

There are many reasons why someone may want to put a value on the equity of a company:

- One company looking to take over another or to merge with that other company will need to know what that company is worth. Even if that company is quoted on a recognized stock exchange, there will be a need to consider whether the quoted market price of the company shares is realistic.
- An individual looking to buy shares in an unquoted company.
- When an unquoted company wishes to float on a stock market it will need to set a price for its equity shares.
- When shares are transferred between people either in lifetime or on death, then a value of those shares is needed for inheritance tax purposes.

Putting a value on the equity of a company is not an exact science. The best we can achieve is a range of possible prices between the minimum that a seller is prepared to accept and the maximum that a buyer is prepared to pay. There are many ways of arriving at estimates of these minimum and maximum values, and this chapter deals with four of the more commonly used approaches.

9.1 Asset-based valuation

Some buyers will buy shares in a company in an effort to gain control of its assets. In the event of a company going into liquidation, the value of its assets will determine how much, if anything, the shareholders will get for their shares.

It is not a straightforward exercise to put a value on the net assets of a company. The financial statements value assets at their 'book' value. This will usually be their cost less, for non-current assets, any related depreciation. These valuations are unlikely to reflect the current value of those assets.

Possible methods of valuation include:

- historic cost basis (book value);
- replacement cost basis;
- realizable value – what they could be sold for;
- going concern basis – what the assets are worth in use to the business.

9.1.1 Minimum asset value

The minimum value that would be applied to the net assets of a company would be based on the minimum that the owners of that company would accept. If it is assumed that the owners want to sell, then the minimum value of the assets of the company would be based on how much the assets could be sold for, less the value of any liabilities that had to be settled. This would be equivalent to the liquidation value of the company, although it may not require the costs of using a liquidator.

The company will know the value of its liabilities and should be able to estimate fairly accurately the value of any current assets. Inventory can sometimes be difficult to value and in a forced sale (as in liquidation) items may sell for less than cost. Companies that are closing down may have to offer discounts on what their customers owe or offer other compensation if they are not going to be able to fulfil any after-sales service once the company has been closed down.

Putting a value on non-current assets is much more problematic. It is often difficult to sell assets such as shop fittings, and there may be a very limited market for second-hand machinery. Specialist estate agents should be able to put a realistic value on any land and buildings if they are owned, but selling on or transferring leasehold premises can be very difficult. The biggest problem, however, is to put a value on any intangible assets that the company has, especially goodwill.

It would be very difficult to sell goodwill without selling the company as a going concern. There have been instances of companies selling their brand names for significant sums (Cadbury's received a very large payment from Premier Foods in 1990 when they sold them the rights to the name 'Smash' when they stopped making that product).

The difference between the value of similar companies with similar assets is sometimes described as the 'intellectual capital' and there is a theoretical approach to putting a value on this.

Example 9.1

JOH Ltd has average pre-tax earnings of £66m and net assets valued at £230m in its financial statements. The industry achieves an average return on net assets of 15 per cent, companies pay tax at 30 per cent and investors expect a 10 per cent return on their investment in that industry.

- Expected return of JOH Ltd = 15 per cent × £230m = £34.5m.
- Actual return is £66m.
- Giving an excess return before tax of £66m − £34.5m = £31.5m.
- This gives a post-tax excess return of £31.5m − 30 per cent = £22.05m.
- This excess return is taken to be the return on the 'intellectual capital' of the company and is equivalent to an asset worth £220.5m (giving a 10 per cent return of £22.05m).
- This would give a possible valuation for the company of £230m + £220.5m = £450.5m.

9.1.2 Maximum asset value

The maximum value would be the maximum that a buyer would be prepared to pay. If a buyer could replace all the assets of a company for less than the company owners require for the sale of their business, the buyer would simply buy the replacement assets.

This would not be as easy as it may seem. There would be the following problems:

- Are the same assets available and will they be in the same condition? Often replacement decisions involve replacing old assets with new ones.
- Can the intangible assets, especially goodwill, be replaced?
- If a buyer does set up a separate company with similar assets, there will be increased competition in the industry and potentially lower returns.

The financial statements of a company will not help us to compute asset-based valuations as there will be no disclosure of any realizable or replacement values for the assets of that company. The financial statements will give details of what assets are controlled by a company and from the information disclosed we will be able to estimate the average age of those assets. This will then help the person to find other values from other sources.

Example 9.2

The average age of the assets of a company can be estimated using the information disclosed in the financial statements:

- The useful life of each class of assets is disclosed in the 'accounting policies', which are usually found in the notes to the financial statements.
- The cost and depreciation to date are also disclosed in the notes.
- If the cost of machinery is £120m and the depreciation to date is £30m, the assets have had, on average, 25 per cent of their life.
- If machinery is being written off over eight years, then the machines are, on average, two years old.

Unfortunately, estimating the age of assets is not as simple in practice as in the above example. Companies often group assets together that have different expected useful lives and simply disclose a range for that group of assets. Tesco plc have tangible assets (excluding premises) that have lives ranging from nine years to fifty years, and the range for Next plc for similar assets is from two to twenty-five years.

9.2 Dividend-based valuation

A share in a company does not have a predetermined life and can be assumed to continue in perpetuity. Over the life of that share the return can be measured by the dividends that are paid to the shareholder.

The 'dividend valuation model' gives an estimated value for a share, assuming that the dividends paid will grow at a constant rate.

$$P_0 = d_0(1 + g)/(K_e - g)$$

Where:

- P_0 is the current price of a share;
- d_0 is the current dividend;
- g is the rate of growth expected for future dividends;
- K_e is the cost of equity for shareholders, which is the same as the return required by those shareholders, and this will reflect the risks faced by the company.

Example 9.3

- Jim Ltd has just paid a dividend of 20p per share.
- Dividends are expected to grow at 5 per cent per annum.
- Shareholders require a return of 15 per cent.
- The company has 5m shares in issue (so total current dividends = £1m).
- Using the model described above:
  - $P_0 = (20 \times 1.05)/(0.15 - 0.05) = 210p = £2.10$
  - giving a value for the company of £10.5m (£2.10 × 5m).

This model has the following practical problems:

- Estimating future growth. Just because dividends have grown in the past is no guarantee for future growth. Some companies do have stable dividend policies with growth rates close to a constant, but there are many exceptions. The table below (9.1), extended from the one first seen in Chapter 6, highlights this point.

Table 9.1

	Next plc pence	Dividend growth (g) %	Tesco plc pence	g %	Marks & Spencer plc pence	g %	Game Group plc pence	g %	Wolseley plc pence	g %
2007	49		9.64		18.3		2.93		117.5	
2008	55	12	10.90	13	22.5	23	4.40	50	40.8	−65
2009	55	0	11.96	10	17.8	−21	5.50	25	0	−100
2010	66	20	13.05	9	15.0	−16	5.78	5	0	0
2011	78	18	14.46	11	17.0	13	5.78	0	45.0	∞

- Some companies do not pay dividends. If we put 0 for the current dividend into this model we get 0 for the value of the company.

- If a company has very high growth, we get unusual answers. If g is greater than K_e, we get a negative value for the company shares.
- The model assumes that we can estimate the return required by shareholders (K_e), that it will be constant going forward and that it will be the same for all shareholders.

9.2.1 Synergy

Synergy is a term used to explain why the present value of two or more merged companies can be greater than the sum of the present values of the individual companies. It is sometimes described as the '2 + 2 = 5' effect.

Synergy arises for many reasons:

- Operating economies of scale – the larger, merged company may have greater buying power and be able to negotiate cheaper prices for goods and services that are bought in.
- Shared knowledge – the companies merging can all benefit from the research and development activities of each company.
- Diversification – companies that face different risks may have a lower overall risk when combined, this will reduce the expected returns and the cost of equity.
- Quality of earnings improves – this can arise especially where companies merge and reduce the competition in an industry or where vertical integration (a company takes over its supplier or its customer) occurs.
- There may be greater prospects for future growth, especially as larger companies often find it easier to raise finance.
- There may be more strategic opportunities through shared customers or access to new markets.

Example 9.4

- Sarah Ltd is planning a takeover bid for Jim Ltd (see Example 9.3 opposite).
- Sarah Ltd has just paid a total dividend of £2m.
- Growth of 5 per cent is expected and shareholders in Sarah Ltd require a return of 12 per cent, which will not be affected by the takeover.
- If the takeover is successful, it is estimated that synergies will result in earnings growth that will increase the total dividend paid out, in current terms, by £0.25m.
- Sarah Ltd before the takeover:

  – P_0 (for the company) = (2m × 1.05)/(0.12 – 0.05) = £30m

- Sarah Ltd after the takeover:

  – Combined dividend payment = £2m + £1m + £0.25m = £3.25m
  – P_0 (for the combined company) = (3.25m × 1.05)/(0.12 – 0.05) = £48.75m
  – An increase of £18.75m as a result of the takeover. In the example above Jim Ltd was valued at only £10.5m.

- Using this model, the shareholders of Jim Ltd may be willing to sell for £2.10 per share, a possible minimum value. The shareholders in Sarah Ltd may be prepared to pay up to £3.75 per share (£18.75m/5m shares), a possible maximum value.

9.3 Present value of future cash flows

The dividend valuation model gives a valuation based on the present value of future dividends. An alternative approach is to use future cash flows rather than dividends.

Using the present value of future cash flows is a common technique used in practice by companies to evaluate long-term projects. The approach can also be used for 'takeover projects' that take account of any increased cash flows due to synergies.

Current cash flows are shown in company financial statements and this data can be used to estimate future cash flows of both individual and combined companies. The approach has the same problems as the dividend approach in that it has to be assumed that any growth achieved will be constant and that we can estimate a constant return required by all shareholders. This approach may be more reliable in practice for companies that do not pay dividends or do not have stable dividend policies.

9.4 Earnings-based valuations

Valuing a company on the basis of its expected future earnings is a very popular approach in practice. The price earnings ratio was first covered in Chapter 6 and is calculated as follows:

PE = Market price per share/EPS

Rearranging that formula gives:

Market price per share = EPS × PE ratio

The EPS that is used should reflect the future sustainable earnings. That means removing anything included in its calculation that is unlikely to apply in the future. It is not necessary to adjust for future growth in earnings as that should be covered by the PE ratio as described in the earlier chapter.

This approach can be used for unquoted companies that do not have their own PE ratio. In those cases it is normal to take the average PE for the industry with a percentage reduction of up to 50 per cent to reflect the size of the unquoted company, the lack of marketability of its shares and the potential that it has for growth.

Example 9.5

ABC plc is considering a takeover bid for XYZ Ltd. Both companies are in the same industry, but ABC is a much larger company, with a PE ratio of 16. XYZ has current, sustainable earnings of 50p per share.

A possible valuation would be:

- Price per share = EPS × Adjusted PE ratio for the industry
- Price per share = 50p ×16 × 60 per cent = £4.80

This is a rather simplistic method, but it is widely used. It is commonly referred to when a company is floated to give an indication of anticipated growth. Famously, when Planet

Hollywood was launched in the UK, its shares were priced based on anticipated initial earnings and a PE ratio of 100, such was the expectation of growth. In this case, however, the growth was not achieved. The use of PE ratios to value companies involved in takeovers can lead to greater gains than may be expected.

Example 9.6

Big plc is planning a takeover of Small plc:

- Big plc has earnings of £20m and a PE ratio of 20, giving a market capitalization of £400m (20m × 20).
- Small plc has earnings of £10m and a PE ratio of 15, giving a market capitalization of £150m (10m × 15).
- Combining Big plc and Small plc with no synergy should (in theory) give a combined market capitalization of £550m (400m + 150m) and combined earnings of £30m, implying a new (weighted average) PE ratio of 18.33.
- It is possible that investors may perceive little change in the prospects of Big plc and may apply its PE ratio of 20 to all the combined earnings, giving a new value of £600m (30m × 20), an instant gain of £50m (600m – 550m).
- This effect does happen in practice and is referred to as 'bootstrapping'.

An alternative to valuing a company as a multiple of earnings would be to use a multiple of the annual sales, or turnover, of the company. This approach is common for small companies in the service sector. If a qualified accountant with a small practice wishes to retire, his business is unlikely to have significant assets, so the value is likely to be based on a multiple of the annual fee income he receives from his clients – the multiple in these cases can be as low as 1.

9.5 Synergy – what synergy?!

In 1998, German car manufacturer Daimler-Benz acquired its American competitor Chrysler for $36m. Being in the same industry they expected significant savings due to synergy between the companies:

- Sales synergy – from the sharing of sales facilities.
- Cost synergy – reduced supplier prices, shared technology, shared research and development.
- Financial synergy – as well as other savings Daimler-Benz hoped to make use of tax losses that Chrysler brought to the company that would reduce to overall tax bill.

In 2007, Daimler-Benz sold their shares in Chrysler for only $5m. The loss to shareholders relating to this takeover was equivalent to the company giving away 4,000 cars per month for the period of share ownership! The synergies were not realized, and there were other problems due to language and cultural differences that led to very difficult working relationships.

When trying to decide on the likely success of a merger or takeover, investors should try to evaluate the following:

- The impact of a change in management for the company being taken over.
- The likelihood that any expected synergies will be realized.
- The compatability of the systems operated by the two companies.
- The value of key members of staff – will the enlarged company be able to keep them?

9.6 Defensive tactics

What can a company do when it is faced with a hostile takeover bid? There are various actions that companies can take either to prevent a bid in the first place or to try to persuade shareholders not to sell their shares to that particular bidder.

- Issue a statement to shareholders that gives a more realistic value of the assets of the company than is shown in the latest financial statements as well as issuing forecasts of attractive future profits and dividends.
- If the bidding company is already a major player in the industry, the target company could approach the government to prevent the takeover on the grounds that it would create an unfair or uncompetitive market. Tesco plc were prevented, by the UK government, from buying the Safeway chain of supermarkets because it was felt that the takeover would give them close to a monopoly position in that market (Safeway eventually became part of Morrisons).
- Seek a 'white knight' to rescue them. This can arise when the target company needs to be taken over but does not want to be taken over by a particular bidder (the 'black knight'), so they seek another buyer that they would not mind being taken over by (their 'white knight'). In some situations, the friendly bidder is only required to buy a significant minority stake to put off the hostile bidder. This friendly bidder is then referred to as a 'white squire'.
- The 'Pac-Man' defence. A company faced by a hostile takeover starts to buy the stock of the bidding company in an attempt to create a reverse hostile takeover.
- Poison pills. Companies may attempt to create a situation where certain events would be activated if the company was taken over. An example might be that all of their debt had to be repaid. Many of these 'poison-pill' activities are illegal and very few ever succeed.

9.7 Finance for takeovers

One company buying shares in another company can either pay for them in cash (a 'cash' bid) or offer the target company shareholders shares in the bidding company (a 'paper' bid).

Companies with large cash balances disclosed under current assets in their financial statements are often considered to be about to bid for another company. This fuels speculation, which could inflate the price of target company shares. Raising a large amount of debt could also increase speculation. Bidding companies planning to use debt finance for their bid often try to arrange a 'line of credit' to be used if their bid is successful. This can prevent, or at least delay, some of the speculation.

Factors affecting the use of cash or paper include:

- Impact on EPS. If a lot of new shares are issued to finance the bid, EPS can be significantly diluted and this will not be popular with shareholders.
- The cost of debt (interest rate) faced by the company.
- If cash is used that the company already has, the shareholders will expect a return on that cash, which may be greater than the cost of using debt.
- The impact on gearing of issuing new debt or new share capital.
- The issue of shares could affect who controls the company. If a shareholder owns 60m of the 100m shares in issue, that shareholder controls the company (>50 per cent of the shares). If 30m new shares are issued to the shareholders of a target company, that shareholder now has 60m out of 130m (approximately 46 per cent) and has therefore lost control.
- Taxation. If shareholders sell for cash they will be liable, in the UK, for capital gains tax. If they accept shares, those gains would not be realized until the shares are sold. The gains are said to be 'rolled forward'.
- The availability of debt.
- Having sufficiently authorized, but not yet issued, share capital to meet the demands of the target company shareholders. This will be affected by the current market price of those shares.

Problems

The directors of Georgina plc are considering the acquisition of the entire share capital of Grace Ltd. See balance sheet overleaf.

- There have been no changes to the issued share capital in the last five years.
- Estimated replacement cost of non-current assets is £725k and inventories £550k. Estimated realizable value of non-current assets is £450k and for inventories it is £570k.
- Shareholders in Georgina plc expect a 9 per cent return and shareholders in Grace Ltd expect a 12 per cent return from their investments.
- The current PE ratio for Georgina plc is 12. Quoted companies in the same industry as Grace Ltd have an average PE ratio of 10, but they are much larger than Grace Ltd.

1   Estimate the value of the total equity of Grace Ltd using as many different methods as possible.

2   Explain the limitations of each valuation.

3   Suggest a range within which the purchase price is likely to be agreed.

Balance sheet of Grace Ltd as at 28 February 2012

	£000	£000
Non-current assets (NBV)		650
Current assets		
Inventories	516	
Receivables	745	
Cash	159	1,420
		2,070
Current liabilities		
Payables		1,616
		454
Share capital		50
Retained earnings		404
Equity		454

Summarized income statements

	2008 £000	2009 £000	2010 £000	2011 £000	2012 £000
Profit (after tax) but before non-recurring items	30	69	49	48	53
Non-recurring items	3	(2)	(6)	(9)	(1)
	33	67	43	39	52
Dividends	21	23	25	25	25
Added to reserves	12	44	18	14	27

Further information:

Activities

1   For the companies you have analysed in earlier chapters, apply the valuation techniques described in this chapter and compare the answers with the current market value.
2   Research some examples of takeovers and review the financial statements of the companies involved before and after the takeover. Were synergies achieved?

Discussion topic

What other information could be included in the annual report of a company that would help a user to reach a realistic valuation of that company?

Chapter 10

What do financial statements not tell the users?

Most companies prepare financial statements to meet the minimum disclosure requirements set by accounting standards and the laws of the country. Content that does not have to be disclosed is unlikely to be included. The management of a company do not use the published financial statements to make their economic decisions, they base their decision-making on the 'management' accounts.

10.1 Financial accounts versus management accounts

The key differences between financial and management accounts are shown in Table 10.1 (see overleaf).

Management accounts have become a very valuable tool that enables managers to plan and control their companies. By comparing what has happened in a month with what was expected to happen that month, managers can see whether or not they are in control. If something is going wrong, corrective action can be taken before it is too late.

The detailed information in the management accounts of a company would be very useful to users in making good economic decisions. Most users are probably more interested in current and future performance and position than they are in the past performance and position of a company.

10.2 The balanced scorecard

The management of a company need information that covers all areas of performance in an objective and unbiased way. The 'balanced scorecard' aims to provide this information for managers using indicators that are divided into four different perspectives:

- The customer perspective.
- The internal business processes perspective.
- The learning and growth perspective.
- The financial perspective.

Only one of the four perspectives uses financial data and the information required by the other three cannot be obtained from the financial statements of the company concerned. Taking a balanced scorecard approach has the key advantage that it considers both internal and external factors and this is crucial to improving the understanding of

Table 10.1

Financial accounts	Management accounts
Are a legal requirement and are published	Are not a legal requirement and are not published
Have to be prepared using a standard format and standard terminology	Have no standard format and can use terminology that is probably more suited to that company
Are only produced annually and take several weeks or months to prepare	Most companies produce monthly management accounts (though some have moved to weekly) and they have to be ready within a day or two of the end of the month
Contain minimum disclosure	Contain maximum disclosure
Only concerned with financial data	Concerned with quantitative and qualitative data
Show previous year as a comparison	Compares current period previous periods and the budget, considering the month or week and the year to date
Are produced in a consolidated format combining all the activities of a company	Show detailed results for each division, product, service, etc.

key issues. Rather than just looking at the results of the company in the financial statements, this approach links together financial and non-financial measures that are related to the key elements of that company's overall strategy.

10.2.1 The customer perspective

The aim in this section is to consider what is important to customers and to measure if the company is delivering what their customers want. Management need to consider what existing and new customers value from their company and they need to consider targets that matter to customers based on factors such as selling prices, quality, delivery times, and so on.

For example, the customers of a supermarket want quality products at low prices and they expect the supermarket not to run out of the products they want to buy. The supermarket needs to measure how well they satisfy the needs of their customers:

- They might measure quality by looking at the proportion of goods retuned by customers.
- They can compare prices of like goods with their competitors – this is something that UK supermarkets do extensively, some offering refunds if their products are not the cheapest.
- They could also record how often they were unable to supply a product to a customer due to being out of stock.

The performance measures referred to above are clearly important to the success of a supermarket, but they cannot be found from information in the financial statements.

Other possible measures of the customer perspective include:

- The need to stay ahead of competitors might be measured by the proportion of sales made from new products.
- To measure responsiveness a company could calculate the proportion of deliveries made on time.
- A company may set a goal of becoming the preferred supplier to important customers. This could be measured by the share of each customer's purchases that they meet.

10.2.2 The internal business process perspective

It is important that a company excels at the processes that are crucial to the achievement of financial and customer objectives. Companies can achieve this by improving internal processes and decision-making.

Manufacturing excellence could be measured by a combination of the time taken to manufacture a product, the cost of producing it and the amount of waste resulting from the production process. A company that can produce a product of equal quality, when compared to a competitor product, at a lower cost and with less damage to the environment is likely to be in a strong position.

Other possible measures of the internal business process perspective include:

- A company could measure its technological capability by comparing its manufacturing configuration with that of its competitors.
- Design productivity could be measured by engineering efficiency.
- The rate of introduction of new products can be assessed by comparing actual introductions achieved relative to the number of new introductions planned.

10.2.3 The learning and growth perspective

Stakeholders in a company will expect to see continued improvements and the creation of future value. The learning and growth perspective considers a company's capacity to maintain its competitive position through the acquisition of new skills and the development of new products and services.

A successful company is unlikely to remain successful if it does not maintain or improve the skills of its staff and ensure that it gets new products to market ahead of its competitors. Maintaining the skills of employees is sometimes measured by the amount of money spent on training courses. It is important that companies consider the quality of this training by measuring any change in the efficiency or effectiveness of the staff sent on the courses.

Further measures for the learning and growth perspective might relate to the time taken to develop new products or services, and how long it takes to get those products or services to the market relative to their competitors.

10.2.4 The financial perspective

The financial perspective looks at the traditional measures that were covered in Chapters 3 to 6. Profitability, liquidity, gearing and shareholder value can be calculated to measure the ability of a company to survive (cash flow), succeed (growth) and prosper (increased market share and ROCE).

10.2.5 Problems with the balanced scorecard approach

Companies using a balanced scorecard approach must take care to avoid these pitfalls:

- Some of the measures of performance could conflict – spending more on research or training is good for the learning and growth perspective, but not good if there are targets to reduce costs in other perspectives.
- It is important not to choose too many measures, only those that really are appropriate should be considered.
- Staff need to be aware of the indicators and understand why they are necessary. Complex indicators can lead to a lot of confusion.
- Balancing the scorecard. To interpret all the measures, it may be necessary to put all the data into an overall perspective. This will bring problems relating to establishing the importance of each measure and the weighting attached to it.

10.3 Non-financial indicators

There are problems in making economic decisions based only on financial performance indicators based on the financial statements of a company:

- They concentrate on too few variables.
- They ignore factors such as quality, which are very important.
- They may measure success but are unlikely to ensure success.

There is a growing emphasis on the importance of using non-financial indicators. This is mainly due to changes that have taken place in competitive and manufacturing environments and changes in cost structures, which can now be very complex.

Non-financial indicators are defined as measures of performance based on non-financial information and are used to monitor and control without any accounting input. Some of the more commonly used examples are shown in Table 10.2.

10.4 Accounting for inflation

Financial statements are prepared, as described in Chapter 1, using the 'historic cost' concept. Transactions are recorded at their original cost and no attempt is made to reflect the current value of what has been purchased. This can cause problems for companies if there is a period of relatively high inflation.

Table 10.2

Area being assessed	Performance measures
Quality of service – useful in a range of companies, including restaurants and car dealerships	Proportion of repeat bookings Customer waiting time Proportion of on time deliveries Number of complaints received
Production performance – very useful in most manufacturing companies	Set-up times Number of suppliers Days inventory held Output per employee Material wastage Labour utilization Budget output achieved Proportion of output to be reworked
Marketing effectiveness	Market share – current and trend Growth in sales volume Customer visits per salesperson Budget sales volume achieved Number of (new) customers
Personnel/human resources – particularly useful in service industries	Number of complaints received Staff turnover (a key indicator of motivation) Absenteeism – days lost Training time per employee

Example 10.1

- Two traders sell the same product and at the start of an accounting period each has inventory that has cost £20,000 and £5,000 in the bank.
- Mr Finacc (a financial accountant) is approached by a customer who offers him £24,000 for all the goods he has in his inventory. He checks his records and sees that the goods originally cost £20,000, so he agrees to the sale and banks the cash received. This transaction means that Mr Finacc has made a profit of £4,000 (£24,000 – £20,000) and he now has £29,000 (£24,000 + £5,000) in his bank account. He then calls his supplier to replenish his inventory. The price of this product has gone up due to inflation and the same quantity now costs £28,000, which Mr Finacc duly pays, leaving him with £1,000 in the bank.
- Following these transactions, Mr Finacc will show a profit of £4,000 in his income statement and in his balance sheet he will show a growth in assets from £25,000 (inventory of £20,000 and cash of £5,000) to £29,000 (inventory of £28,000 and cash of £1,000).
- The other trader, Mr Manacc (a management accountant), meets the same customer and is offered the same deal. Instead of checking the original cost of the goods, he calls his supplier to find out their replacement cost. This information leads him to turn down the sale. This means that Mr Manacc shows no profit in his income statement and no growth in his assets in his balance sheet.

- Which trader is now in the best financial position?
- If the product being traded has not changed and is not perishable, then Mr Manacc is in a better financial situation as both traders have the same inventory items and he has £4,000 more cash in his bank account. It is important not to sell goods for less than it costs to replace them.
- Mr Finacc may have made a profit and grown his assets but he will run out of cash and end up in liquidation if he continues to make similar decisions.

Example 10.1 highlights the problem in judging a company on financial ratios based on financial accounting rules. A company can make profits for many years but still run out of cash and therefore become insolvent, especially in periods of high inflation.

Following a period of high inflation in the UK in the late 1970s and early 1980s, accounting bodies tried to find a solution to the problem by producing financial statements that took into account adjustments for inflation. Unfortunately, the suggested change to 'current cost accounting' did not take off because it made the financial statements too complicated for a lot of users.

Problems

1   Which balance scorecard perspectives are being measured by the following ratios?

   (a) ROCE.
   (b) Current ratio.
   (c) Financial gearing ratio.
   (d) EPS.
   (e) Customer returns as a percentage of sales.
   (f) Amount spent on training per employee.
   (g) Proportion of products made that are rejected by quality control department.

2   Suggest some possible performance measures for the following:

   (a) A company has recently spent £10m on new IT equipment.
   (b) A football team buys a new player for £35m.
   (c) An advertising campaign.
   (d) A decision to relocate.
   (e) A decision to outsource production to another country.
   (f) The performance of a credit control department.
   (g) The success of a recently developed new product.
   (h) The success of a merger or takeover.

Activity

Do financial statements meet their objective? Using the data collected in the activities from all the earlier chapters, based on the financial statements of the companies that you have researched, can you make an economic decision?

(a) As an investor, would you buy shares in those companies?
(b) As a bank manager, would you lend the company money?
(c) As a supplier, would you give credit to the company?
(d) Would you be happy to join the company as an employee?

Discussion topics

1 If a company prepares management accounts and financial accounts for the same period, will they show the same overall profit?
2 Should more non-financial data be disclosed in the annual report of companies? If so, what data should be disclosed?

Index